"I simply wasn't prepared for the power and personal impact that *Navigating Life with More Than Enough* had on me. Todd DeKruyter unpacks the problems of wealth with a personal transparency and humility that disarms and engages. With conviction and grace, I found myself moving from confession to liberation, all in the course of a single book. Regardless of the size of your balance sheet, this is a trustworthy guide through the challenges of wealth."

  **Dan Wolgemuth**, President/CEO, Youth For Christ USA; author, *The Monday Memo, Fragments, and Give Life*

"Financial resources are a blessing, yet they can have profound, unintended consequences. Todd DeKruyter provides a vision and practical tools for understanding and managing our relationship with finances. He begins where we all should begin—with the core essentials of our heart. I highly recommended this book to those seeking to be good stewards of all the resources they earn, inherit, and are blessed to receive."

  **Beverly Y. Upton**, Chief Executive Officer, Haggai Institute

"I have had the privilege of consulting and counseling thousands of individuals and couples, many with significant wealth. Having wealth is not wrong, but it does create many problems. In my experience, the biggest issues come in the second and subsequent generations. Todd DeKruyter is extremely qualified to speak to this subject as an heir who has dealt with all the issues he describes in this book. I recommend it highly for those who have wealth to transfer, the recipients of inherited wealth, and especially for those who are in the financial services world who deal with the wealthy. A great and much needed book."

  **Ron Blue**, Founder, Ron Blue Institute; author, *Splitting Heirs*

"Todd DeKruyter peels off wealth's protective sheen to reveal what lies beneath. His personal experience with wealth and his time as an advisor inform this investigation of the challenges and disappointments that can surprisingly accompany affluence. His prescription is a huge dose of wisdom. I wish someone had handed this book to me when I was 23!"

  **John Cortines**, Executive Vice President, Emerging Leaders, Generous Giving; co-author, *God and Money: How We Discovered True Riches at Harvard Business School*

"As a child who grew up in affluence, Todd has a unique perspective to share with readers. His book is full of thoughtful questions, honest personal reflections, and valuable wisdom. I commend this book to anyone seeking to wisely steward excess resources rather than acquiesce to the prevailing culture of bigger, better, faster makes you happy."

**Todd Harper**, President, Generous Giving; author, *Abundant*

"I love the way Todd defines affluence as having more than enough. He lays out an honest assessment of how affluence presents challenges for all of us, both relationally and spiritually. Todd speaks candidly to those challenges out of his own life experiences. There is no cookie-cutter formula here. There is wise and transparent guidance for those who want to find true life in the midst of affluence."

**Patrick Johnson**, Founder, GenerousChurch

"Money can create complexity and idols that no one would wish on their worst enemy, while simultaneously being a powerful tools if we submit ourselves to God's leading. This book is filled with practical insights and wisdom that can only be described as a gift from the Lord. This is certainly one of the best books I have read on the topic of stewardship and the influence that money has."

**Paul Larson**, Founder and Managing Partner, Larson Financial Group; Principal, Larson Financial Foundation

"Todd writes with a personal knowledge of both the blessings and the curses of being surrounded by wealth. The breadth of his knowledge vastly exceeds his number of years. He freely quotes from both the Bible and a plethora of thought leaders, making this short book a virtual compendium of wisdom and guidance on how to and how not to handle the material possessions the Lord entrusts to you. You will find this book both enlightening and inspiring. Reading it will definitely be time well spent!"

**E. G. "Jay" Link**, Whole Life Stewardship Coach; Family Wealth Counselor; author, *To Whom Much is Given*

"This book provides extraordinary insight into the very serious issues facing those who have been entrusted with more than enough. DeKruyter approaches the subject with wisdom, humility, practicality, and personal experience. I found particularly thought-provoking the chapters describing the dangerous impact affluence can have on our children and what we can do as parents to help them handle money well."

**Larry Powell**, Powell Family Enterprises, LLC

# NAVIGATING LIFE WITH MORE THAN ENOUGH

*Todd DeKruyter* (signature)

**Todd DeKruyter**

*Navigating Life with More Than Enough*
Copyright © 2016 by Todd DeKruyter

All rights reserved. No part of this publication may be reproduced, stored in a retrieval system, or transmitted in any form by any means, including photocopying, recording, or other electronic or mechanical methods, without the prior permission of the author, except as provided for by USA copyright law.

**Library of Congress Cataloging-in-Publication Data**

DeKruyter, Todd, author.
  Navigating life with more than enough / by Todd DeKruyter.
    p. cm.
  Includes bibliographical references. | Fishers, IN: Weaver Crosspoint, 2017.
  ISBN 978-0-9864125-0-9 (pbk.) | 978-0-9864125-1-6 (ebook) |
  LCCN 2016917563
  1._LCSH Rich people--Conduct of life. 2. Money--Philosophy. 3. Finance, Personal. 4. Money--Psychological aspects. 5. Wealth--Psychological aspects. 6. Success in children. 7. Wealth--Religious aspects--Christianity. 8. Rich people--Religious life. 9. Wealth--Moral and ethical aspects. I. Title
  LCC HB251 .D45 2017
  305.5234--dc23
                                                                                            2016917563

All scripture quotations, unless otherwise indicated, are taken from *The Holy Bible, English Standard Version*, copyright © 2001 by Crossway Bibles, a division of Good News Publishers. Used by permission. All rights reserved.

Cover design: Kristen Williams
Interior design: Carson Cheatham

Print ISBN: 978-0-9864125-0-9
EBook ISBN: 978-0-9864125-1-6

## CONTENTS

| | |
|---|---|
| Acknowledgements | 9 |
| Prologue | 15 |
| 1. The Difference Money Makes<br>*How Do We Fight to Live a Legacy Worth Remembering?* | 26 |
| 2. Money and Your Heart<br>*8 Money Myths and Why Our Legacy Story Matters* | 41 |
| 3. Success, Achievement, and Significance<br>*Do You Fear Death without Significance?* | 60 |
| 4. Oh, the Lies We Tell Ourselves<br>*Why Don't the Affluent Really Talk about Money?* | 81 |
| 5. Attacking the Root<br>*How Do We Get to the Heart of the Matter?* | 98 |
| 6. The Flip Side of Affluence<br>*15 Things Affluence Does to Us that Don't Make the News* | 117 |
| 7. The Flip Side of Affluence for Our Children<br>*How Does Affluence Impact our Children?* | 137 |
| 8. Helping our Kids Handle Money Well<br>*Practical Suggestions for Keeping Our Kids from Entitlement* | 155 |
| 9. Beautiful Tension<br>*Do People Love You or Just Your Stuff?* | 176 |
| 10. Community for the Affluent<br>*How Can We Keep Judgment, Envy, and Jealousy at Bay?* | 195 |

Epilogue   219

Appendix A - The Faith Dilemma   221
*So if Jesus isn't your deal, should you read this?
Why faith might become a big issue as you become
more affluent.*

Appendix B – Writing Your Family Legacy Story   235
*Tips and suggestions for digging into your past and
facing your family's future together*

## ACKNOWLEDGEMENTS

The old adage about the turtle on the fencepost is true here. "If you see a turtle on top of the fencepost, you know he didn't get there by himself; someone put him there." I've had many people who have spoken into my life and so much help to write this book. I'd like to thank those who have contributed to my finally getting my thoughts down on paper.

To Janelle, my wife, my partner, my true love, my best friend, who has been of incalculable value as I've navigated these waters. She has been a constant support and critic where needed and, most of all, she has been unaffected by money's ugly pull on her heart. I would be a much different person had she not been daily by my side as we do life together.

To my mother and father, Jim and Barb DeKruyter, who taught me too much to name. But with respect to wealth, you've lived out the truths that money isn't everything, loving people is crucial, and humility is beautiful. To my brothers and sisters-in-law, John and Mel, Paul and Krissy, and Jeff and Cheryl—you've done well with much and have kept my heart in check in more ways than you know.

To those people I've interviewed and talked with, your insights have been so critical. Thank you. Larry Powell, I love your boldness to speak truth into my life and into the affluent friends you see regularly. Ron Blue, I love your leadership to giving biblically wise financial advice. David Wills, I love your wisdom and optimism for the future. Dan Wolgemuth, I love your learning spirit and thirst for ministering to the affluent. Wayne Huizenga, Jr., I love your passion to encourage the affluent toward significance. David VanderPloeg, I love your commitment to serving ministers and the affluent. Laura Pflug, you are living well and have a contagious excitement for generosity. Dr. John Edmund Haggai, I love your courage for Jesus, your practical advice, and your childlike faith. Jay Link, I love your energy to stir up passion for stewardship. Renee Lockey, I love your passion and honesty. Tim Mohns, I love your style as you lead from an unassuming and authentic spot. Peter Huizenga, I love your wisdom and desire to preserve what needs to be preserved. Todd Harper, I love your discernment and encouragement to stir up true generosity. Janice Worth, you truly are the "startup queen"; thanks for steering me in the right direction. Jack Alexander, I love how you are pushing the wealthy closer to fully surrender Jesus with their whole life. Daryl Heald, you make me want to be more like Jesus.

And to the growing list of people who are too private to let me mention your names in a book, thank you. Your insight, humility, and integrity are inspiring.

To Tim Beldner and Jake Whipp, your accountability, challenge, and encouragement are priceless. You get me to work out, but also to love better. Thank you for your difficult questions, prayers, counsel, and soul-level friendship.

To my editors, Julie Nason Vincent and C. Rebecca Rine, this book wouldn't be coherent without you. Your edits, feedback, and insight have been fabulous. Ladies, you are golden.

To the Useful Group—James Kinnard, Angie Cheatham, Carson Cheatham, and Rachel Poel, thanks for helping me get to print. I've loved your insights, polish, questions, and guidance on this process.

To my early readers, thank you for your perspective, push back, time, and insight. Special thanks to Lauren Oschman, John Cortines, Gretchen Easterday, Barb DeKruyter, Tom Martin, and my dearest Janelle.

To my partners at Larson: Tom Martin, Paul Larson, Tim Beldner, Jeff Larson, Jake Whipp, Rick Frith, Lauren Oschman, Forrest Freidow, and Randy Larson. You have helped me down the path of financial insights and have shown me how it's possible to be a man who loves his family and who can be significant in business at the same time.

To my business coach Ralph Larimer, this book is your fault. I wouldn't have written anything down without your push. Thank you.

To my professors and teachers along the way--from Harvard Business School, Trinity Evangelical Divinity School, Focus Leadership, Huntington University, Summit Ministries, and Kalamazoo Christian—thank you doesn't say enough. You've taught me how to think; I am eternally grateful.

To the "guys" in the office, Jake Stevenson, Cameron Heasley, Jacob Fisher, Ken Stillings, Jake Stone, Jake Fidler, Zach Brown, Sara Israel, Dan Hillen, Emily Wheeler, Gillian Kasser, Matt Harlow, Danielle Gaines, Katie Ward, Christine "it's weird to not say Cici" Humphries, and Steph Jones. (Yes, there have been four Jakes in the office. It has been confusing at times). Your critiques helped me formulate and explain so many of these ideas. And your ability to do your job with excellence allowed me freedom to write. Thank you.

To the one and only, celebrated, legendary, and fabled J. Paul Fridenmaker. A man of mythical renown. If only Shakespeare could write a sonnet to describe how amazing you are, then the words might be enough — your effortless charm, your lavish charisma, your colossal intellect, your crucial acumen, and your thoughtful humor are unparalleled. Even your goatee is soaked in so much wisdom a whole book could be written about it. Your . . . what? Was that too much?

To the Generous Giving Team, thanks for living out how to love people well. Thanks to Todd Harper, David Gonzales, Matt Mancinelli, Julie Wilson, John Cortines, Steve Atkinson, Lacie Stevens, Ladonna Cingilli, Janice Munemitsu, Lacie Stevens, Mac South, Jordan Stone, Lindsey Johnson, Melinda Eller, Spencer Karges, Emily Stadt, Mary Shaw, Kristy Champion, Verne Murray, and Stephen Rolston. I love how well you love people.

To my readers—first, thank you for reading. As you go through the book, you will notice I have referenced many books and articles I have read through the years, along with conferences, sermons, workshops, interviews, and speeches I have had the opportunity to attend. I have made every effort to attribute ideas and quotes as I went along. My concern is that I have read so many things that they all blur together. Also, many people

I have come into contact with through the years share some of the same beliefs, advice, and outlooks. So, please forgive me if you think my attribution is less than complete. I assure you I have made every effort to get it right. Again, my heartfelt thanks to those of you who know you have inspired me, and to those who may not know the impact you have had on my thinking and my life.

## PROLOGUE

### WHY I WROTE THIS BOOK

What do you think of when you think of affluence? What do you think it looks and feels like to be "rich"?

The upsides to affluence are apparent to many people. The degrees, the houses, the cars, the exotic vacations. Access to almost any convenience you want, when you want it. But the downsides are not as obvious and are rarely discussed. In the pages that follow, my goal is to pull back the curtain on the flip side of wealth. You might even call it the "dark side."

As you read, some of you might push back, saying, "What problems could rich people really have?" Others of you, however, will say to yourselves, "Wow, someone has been reading my mail."

Some of us have the impression "once rich, always rich"—that is, we think that people with wealth were born that way. We think of wealth as something that is inherited. But in reality, 80% of those that are wealthy are the first generation in their family to be wealthy. This tells us two things.

One, this affluence thing is new to the vast majority of those facing it. Many affluent people have little or no experience navigating either the upsides or the downsides of affluence. And even those who do inherit wealth may not have thought about the many ways affluence will impact their decisions and identity.

And two, those "old-money families" are mostly headlines and myths. They do exist, but are not as common as fiction would make them seem. In most research studies, up to 90% of the wealth earned in the first generation to be wealthy is gone by the end of the third. The children of the affluent live with the trappings but miss the values needed to stay, grow, work, and live well in that space.

There are plenty of financial advisors and estate planners who can help you navigate the hard numbers of affluence. There are investment tools, portfolio trackers, asset protection strategies, estate planning techniques, and more to help you manage your money. But what about navigating the flip side of affluence? What does affluence do to your kids? What about understanding how affluence changes the way you see yourself and the way other people see you? What about taking care of the ones you love, not just financially, but relationally?

That is why I have written this book: to help you navigate affluence using more than just your checkbook or a mobile app. Financial planning tools are important. My day job for a decade was a financial planner! They have some good tools. But most of these tools do not account for the way money pulls on our hearts. This is what we are here to explore.

## THE TRAPPINGS OF WEALTH

*Where the Red Fern Grows* by Wilson Rawls is a fabulous book. Its pages tell the tale of the life of a little boy named Billy and his coon dogs, Ann and Dan, as they trap and search for raccoons in a poor segment of the rural Ozark Mountains. It's a genuinely remarkable story.

In one part of the story, Billy builds a raccoon trap. He makes a little hole in the wood and inserts angled nails and a piece of something shiny in the bottom. The idea of the trap is that raccoons like shiny objects. When they put their little paw in and grab onto the little shiny something, their balled-up little fist gets stuck. As long as they hold on to the shiny object, they remain trapped. But since raccoons love shiny things so much, they hold tightly until the hunter comes back.

For many of us, money and the trappings of wealth are the shiny object. The accumulation and preservation of wealth becomes our goal, our pursuit, and even our drive. We think that money will help us address our problems. If only we could afford a better car, a bigger house, or a nicer vacation, our quality of life is bound to improve. Yet after a while, you may start to notice that success and wealth feel more like a trap. Our walls of asset protection and strategies to protect ourselves from getting hoodwinked again were meant to form a castle of protection, but they've turned into a gilded cage. Our unchecked desire and often selfish ambition have led us into a trap.

But like the raccoon who needs to let go of the shiny object, our hearts need to be dragged back from the allure of money. Our tendency is to drive and build, which can be good. Yet how often do we ask tough questions, consider the impact of our choices on our kids, or examine how we are really doing with what we've been entrusted? This book is written to help us see, examine, and potentially change how we look at our stuff and our legacy.

## WHAT DO I MEAN BY "AFFLUENCE"?

Affluence doesn't mean the same thing to everone. It's funny—few of us think of ourselves as affluent or rich, because each of us knows someone else who has more money, more assets, or more connections than we do.

Because of this, I'm not going to offer a specific income level or net worth that categorizes a person as "affluent." Simply put, my definition of affluence is having more than enough.

One reason I don't want to specify a number is that I don't want you to look at this book and say, "Oh, this is for them," that is, for "those people" who have more than me. The truth is, a higher income does change things (like which collectables you buy, where you live, and what mode of transportation you use). But it doesn't change everything. If you have enough or just a little more than enough to get by, you can begin thinking about how affluence affects all of us—and you in particular.

If you are not affluent yourself (perhaps you work with affluent people or are just starting down the path to affluence), I hope you will still read this book. I hope you will try to understand and relate to those who are affluent just a little bit better.

Whether you see yourself as affluent or not, there is always someone more or less affluent than you are. But this book was not written for "everybody else"; or rather, it was written for both them and you. I'd like to encourage you to read it first for you. Think, what do I need to hear?

Feel free to skip or ignore the parts that don't resonate at first read. You'll clearly find some sections that apply to you better than others. But what you think doesn't apply might actually be relevant, either now or in the future. So please, spend some time with each chapter and apply it to your own life.

## WHAT MAKES ME QUALIFIED TO WRITE A BOOK ON NAVIGATING AFFLUENCE?

This book has emerged out of my own struggle with what it means to be affluent and out of countless conversations with 200-plus affluent clients, colleagues, mentors, and family members. At times in this book, I will reference research and the writings of others. But much of this book is my own story—things I have learned along the way and am still learning.

The extended family I come from has started dozens of successful companies, three of which have become Fortune 500 companies. We run hedge funds and charter schools, serve in the military, and work/lead in various industries. At family reunions, some can talk about trusts, companies, jets, and yachts—in the plural.

When it comes to navigating affluence, I have lived this struggle, yet still struggle. So I speak from personal experience. But there's more to it than that. I have also made it a personal mission to broaden my scope beyond my immediate circle by extensively reading pertinent research and literature. I earned my master's degree from Trinity Evangelical Divinity School in Christian Studies, Theology, and Church History. As a Chartered Financial Consultant (ChFC), I have spent a decade advising and learning from hundreds of affluent clients via a financial planning practice and networking with other professionals who primarily serve affluent clients. And I host a podcast where I facilitate discussions that have further shaped my perspective that you find in these chapters.

I am also a husband and a father. My wife of thirteen years, Janelle, and I are parents to four children—two boys and two girls. Whenever I think about money and its pull on our hearts, I am always thinking about it from at least two angles. One has to do with industry and professional life, and the other has to do with personal and family life. The two are intertwined. So my roles as son, brother, husband, and father are just as important as my professional expertise. Perhaps you can relate to this. What we want as individuals, family members, and professionals is sometimes more connected than we realize.

Even with this professional and personal experience, I also am still learning. Picture me as a journeyman alongside you. Many of the ideas in this book are well thought out, researched, field tested, and proven. Others, from my perspective, are still very much in process. I do not speak as someone who knows everything about money and its wily tricks. But I do speak as someone who has reflected on this topic and is struggling on this journey with you.

## SO, WHY THIS BOOK?

I wrote this book because I don't want money to have a hold on your heart. Money can be a good tool or a good servant. But it can so quickly switch into the master role before we are even aware of it. A dairy farmer says, "You don't own a dairy farm; it owns you." Likewise, it's easy to get into a position where you don't have money: it has you. Affluence can affect other areas of life in ways that you might not expect.

I want money to be a help, not a hindrance, in your life. I want you to be free from the love of money and its snares. I hope this book will help you have more meaningful and honest relationships at work, at home, and among friends. I truly believe that by living life and making decisions focused on the long view, each of us can make a better story, a better family, and "take hold of that which is truly life."[1]

This doesn't mean that we are prepared for all the changes that having money can bring. Most of us are so busy earning money that we rarely have time to think about what it is like to be among the "wealthy." Others of us were wealthy even before we were born, but that doesn't mean our parents taught us what to do with wealth. In either case, no matter how or why you are moving toward affluence, I believe you will make better choices and navigate wealth more effectively when you live life in light of your legacy and not just today's cares. What if we could live today in light of how our legacy will be viewed in eternity?

Living life in light of your legacy means taking the big picture into account. It means living a more fulfilling life, not being simply focused on the tyranny of the urgent. It also means taking responsibility for how you navigate (manage, steward, maximize the value of) the blessings you've been given. It's not enough just to take things as they come. This book is designed to help you navigate the murky waters of affluence and to enjoy the journey for all it's worth.

## WHY NOW?

Because today matters. This moment is important. And because navigating affluence today looks different than navigating affluence did just a few years ago.

We live at a unique point in history. We have access to more information than ever before, with media formats that bring the struggles of poverty, its faces and even names, right into our living rooms and onto our phones. The world of poverty is no more than a click away or a short drive to the other side of town. Living with affluence in this setting can make the affluent guilt-ridden. At the least, it's a visible part of the landscape that can't be ignored.

In addition, we are often challenged by the need to live locally in an increasingly globalized context. We encounter much of the world around us through movies, Facebook, televised and online news, Instagram, and Pinterest, none of which are geographically bound. Yet we live locally, in one place, with all its particularities. We hear the best comedians in the world, yet we still need to find our friends' jokes funny. We can access the best storytellers, but daily engage with the stories of our spouses and our kids. All of this can result in a feeling of disconnect from either the local or the global. Or we are unable to understand how the two relate.

Another circumstance that makes this time in history unique is that we find ourselves in the age of digital wealth. Our accounts or net worth are not as readily discernible to the outside observer as, let's say, 200 years ago, when wealth wasn't as easily hidden. Today, we can be very wealthy and not necessarily have to let anyone else know it. We can even be wealthy without ourselves knowing in detail what assets we actually have. With bills paid online and electronic transfer of money leaving no "paper trail," it takes a considerable amount of discipline simply to keep track of our assets—much more to have a concrete grasp on what all of the digital data means, either financially or in terms of our identity.

The issues of globalization and digital wealth pose real challenges to our outlook on life. Mass marketing is oh-so-good at reminding us of what we don't have. The Internet constantly shouts at us about what we may be missing by not buying, experiencing, or displaying the newer, the shinier, and the more glamorous. It also gives us endless opportunities to donate or invest in good causes right here and around the world.

In the midst of all this noise, it is helpful to take a time out to reflect on what really matters about money. Is it the bottom line, or is it something more?

## SOME QUESTIONS AS YOU READ

I am thankful that you've taken a few moments to read through this book. I know your time is valuable, and I hope you find in these pages some of what you are looking for. Before you begin, I want to break you out of a pattern of reading books just like you did in school.

My encouragement to you would be to consider and apply the challenges and insights in these pages. I've tried to capture scriptural insights and hard questions throughout that I've confronted first and now put to you. I urge you to pause and reflect when something catches your attention.

To help you know what to focus on to get the most out of this book and apply it immediately to your life, keep these four questions in mind as you read each chapter:

1. What is working well with how you're currently navigating affluence?

2. What is not working well with how you're currently navigating affluence?

3. What about your struggle with affluence do you find confusing?

4. What do you currently need to change about how you're navigating affluence?

These four questions provide a guiding framework to help you track your responses. In fact, you may benefit from pausing for a moment now to think about your answers to these questions. Jot down a list with your initial responses. Writing your thoughts down will help you see how far you've come as you put into practice the thoughts in these pages.

In many ways, this book is like a nice, big steak. Why? Because steaks are best when they're well marinated. Marinating, which takes time, really brings out the flavor. Actually, this isn't just true of steaks; it's also true of eggplant, tofu, or a Portobello mushroom for my vegetarian friends!

The point is this: As you sit down with this book, please let it marinate, not only through your own thoughts, feelings, and engagement along the way, but also in great conversations with others. The more you reflect on and share these ideas, the more you will benefit from them.

If you believe in God, include Him in the conversation as well. I am a Christian, so God is part of how I think through the issues of wealth. However, the discussions that follow are relevant and beneficial regardless of belief system or worldview.

Let's dive in and journey together through murky, seldom-spoken-about waters of affluence, wealth, and privilege. May we be people who ask difficult questions with humility and unvarnished candor. Let us press into what matters. Let us suppress the lies that draw us away from our calling.

May the adventure ahead draw out a childlike excitement about life. May we love well where it matters most. Let us journey into leaving a legacy that counts.

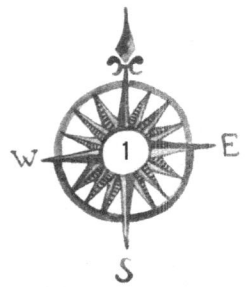

# THE DIFFERENCE MONEY MAKES

*"Many people die with their music still in them. Why is this so? Too often it is because they are always getting ready to live. Before they know it, times run out."*
- Oliver Wendell Holmes -

*"When I was young, I was worried about making enough money. Now that I am old, I worry about making enough difference."*
- Attributed to John D. Rockefeller -

*"The man without a purpose is like a ship without a rudder—a waif, a nothing, a no man. Have a purpose in life, and, having it, throw such strength of mind and muscle into your work as God is giving you."*
- Thomas Carlyle -

It was when I was twelve that I first had the inkling my family was unique. We decided to have a family reunion. Not just any family reunion. We weren't gathering at my grandparents' house or a local park. Instead, the 105 people in my extended family were hopping on a plane to go to Holland. Not the city in Michigan, but the country in Europe.

There were eight kids in my great-grandfather's generation. Of those, five had emigrated to the U.S. and three had stayed in Europe. And now the time had come for the American descendants to reconnect with the homeland.

Until that point in my life, I didn't realize that some people in my family are a big deal. For example, my grandpa's cousin, Wayne Huizenga Sr., catapulted a few companies into the Fortune 100.

The thought of meeting a billionaire might make some people nervous. But when you're twelve, a billion is simply a lot of zeroes. I didn't think much of meeting Wayne at the time. I just saw him as yet another "old dude" at the family reunion. But I did notice how differently adults would react to him.

There were several moments on that trip when it really hit me that something was different about my family. Many of my relatives are very affluent. And people treated them as though they were very affluent. My eyes were beginning to be opened to the impact that money can have.

People change around affluence. My friend tells the story of his neighbor taking over as CEO of a Fortune 100 company. The new CEO had a brief time to ask the old CEO for advice in the transition. The retiring CEO said, "Your jokes are about to get really funny." What did he mean by that? The first piece of advice was about his humor? His comments go deeper than that. He was pointing out that when you move to a position of power, people around you change. When you have money, success, or power, you are treated as though you are smarter, funnier, and better looking.

Due to my family connections, I also got a behind-the-scenes view of generosity. As Americans, we can be oddly private about our giving. As both a family member and a financial advisor, I've seen the full story. I've seen how many of the men and women in my family and outside have given sacrificially, boldly, and with fantastic generosity. And, once you have assets, giving sacrificially is really hard and, unfortunately, often rare.

You may already be forming some ideas about me. But before you categorize me as one of "them," I think it's important for you to know that I find affluence a little weird too. Until I got married, I thought all families were like mine to some extent (perhaps you can relate). But I have seen the behind-the-scenes view of wealth and can speak from experience to the upsides and the downsides.

The research tends to confirm: affluence isn't all it's cracked up to be. Yes, when you're affluent, you can buy a nice house (or maybe even two) and multiple cars. You can go on great trips. You can make special purchases without breaking the bank. But there is so much more to affluence that doesn't hit the papers.

Growing up around money can affect your friendships just as much as it affects your family life. In elementary and high school, my summers were spent at my parent's lake house. I had two groups of friends: a summer group and a rest-of-the-year group. As classes came to an end every June, my school friends and I were always excited for the burden of homework to end and freedom of summer to begin. But there was also always a pause: my friends from school knew I was going to disappear for a few months. As we said our goodbyes, there was always an awkward balance between "we'll miss you" and "you are a little stinker that gets to go have fun at the lake."

I vividly remember the day a group of my year-round friends were hanging out at the lake house. I was sixteen, and we had been close for a few years. That day we were boating, laughing, jet skiing, and playing volleyball. Then there was a lull in the conversation. Joel said, "Todd, I had a blast today! Really, it was fun. But I want you to know, we like you for you—not just your stuff. Don't get me wrong, I could come over here every day and play. But I want you to know, we all talked, and we all like you more than your stuff." How do I know those were his exact words? Because it meant that much to me. He meant it; they meant it; and I remembered it. We didn't hang out there again at the lake for a few months, and we still had fun—without my "stuff."

Here is another vivid memory, one that is not so affirming. While in college, I drove a PT Cruiser. The car didn't have much of an engine, but it looked great (or so I thought). The car actually became a legend in our family, because I used it as part of an atrocious pick-up line when I asked my wife out on our first date. I bumbled through the asking her out part and ended with "and I drive a PT Cruiser," as though this would clearly be a selling point. But I was so nervous, she didn't actually understand what I had asked. Her response was, "Um…did you just ask me out?" Not my most suave moment in dating.

In any case, the "coup de gras" of my ride was its magnetic flames. The car was painted dark blue, and its orange flames were about three feet long. But there are some moments when you don't want flames on your car, so the removable magnets were perfect.

One night a friend borrowed the magnets and lost them. I heard the group walking back into campus talking about how they would tell me that they lost my magnets. The friend who was driving the car said, "Oh, it doesn't matter—he is a spoiled rich kid. Who really cares what he does?" He didn't see me standing there, but I heard him. I remember my cheeks burning with embarrassment and some anger.

So many thoughts went through my head in that moment. I was embarrassed for him and for me. I was mad about my magnets. I wondered how they knew I was a rich kid. I thought I had hidden that part about me pretty well. And what did I do about it? Absolutely nothing. I stood there still unseen, until they passed me.

This is a small memory, but it shows how money (or the perception of money) can have huge ripple effects on relationships. You don't have to look far to find tales of celebrities rolling in dough but suffering daily from shattered marriages and broken relationships. Money enables and causes many of these rifts.

Money's effect on relationships extends beyond disrupting these close ties; it also shapes how we view others. All of us have perceptions about what it means to have (or not have) money.

When I was seventeen, I went on a trip with my church to Ecuador. This was my first real experience with abject poverty. We stayed in the jungle with a tribe of people once known as the Aucas, or now the Waorani people. Some people in their tribe were made famous worldwide when they killed missionaries

Jim Elliot, Nate Saint, Ed McCully, Roger Youderian, and Peter Fleming in the mid-1950s. In the United States, this story was big news. It even made the cover of Life magazine. But by the 1990s, the tribe that had killed Christians had become Christians. Here we were now jumping on a plane to meet them.

On the flight into the jungle, our plane was so small that I had to be weighed to determine my seat. When we arrived in the remote part of the jungle for three days, I was shocked at what I saw. Their home was what I thought of as a "pole barn," a barn without sides, and there were simple hammocks strung from each pole. Forty or so people were living in a home the size of a three-car garage. I remember wondering if these people even knew about the outside world with electricity, airplanes, and cars. Why would they stay here? Were they just lazy?

They led us on a hunting trip in the jungle to get food. We went off in one direction with a guide and saw nothing. But the other group came back with a turkey-like bird for our feast. I think they may have used the American kids and our loud walking to scare the game their way. They had a feast that night, and we ate the whole bird. I remember being grossed out by finding a piece of the throat in my soup.

At the time, my heart was so arrogant and cold to their struggles and their hand-to-mouth existence. Yet here they were treating us with such kindness. They let us sleep in their hammocks while they slept outside on the ground.

I'm embarrassed now about how I felt toward them and how naively I viewed their poverty as their fault. How arrogant I was for thinking I had anything to do with my surroundings—computers, paved roads, and electricity! I thought they were lazy while I was the one who sat around in the summers watching movies and playing on the lake. They were fighting hard every day just to survive.

I could tell you more stories about how affluence has affected me, but honestly, some are too personal, and some aren't fully mine to tell. Perhaps you can think of a few of your own—moments that have made you stop and think about how money affects each of us. It affects how we look at others and how other people look at us. This is true whether we have a lot or a little.

In any case, I tell you these stories not just so that you understand me better, but to point out that wealth is so much more than numbers on a balance sheet. Managing wealth involves more than addressing tax issues, protecting financial assets, and absorbing the latest investment stratgy.

## AFFLUENCE CHANGES THINGS

Most of us recognize that affluence changes things. We know that we judge people's character based on what they do with their money; our expectations change based on our knowledge (or opinion) of a person's net worth.

For instance, a lot of us think that rich people are jerks. But just because you have money doesn't mean that you're a jerk. There are plenty of jerks who are not affluent, and there are plenty of affluent people who aren't arrogant.

At the same time, we also tend to expect that money shouldn't change people. We compliment the rich when we notice, "she didn't forget her roots" or "he remembers where he came from." The people who "forget their roots" or "forget where they came from" are criticized for allowing money to shift their allegiances. But we often make these judgments without knowing the whole story—either where someone came from or where they are going.

## SO WHAT CHANGES WHEN WE HAVE MONEY?

Money and what it affords changes us. Affluence can twist identities, alter decision-making, change the way we view others, and often foster envy and jealousy. Rich people can be astonishingly lonely. And sometimes, the very things we aspire to—wealth, financial security, the ability to give generously—become the very things that cut us off from the people we care about the most.

While we expect wealth to solve our isolation and anxieties, the challenges described by the upper extreme of affluence contradict this. The Atlantic summarized well a study done by Boston College in connection with the Gates Foundation and John Templeton Foundation on the "Super Rich," as they called them.[2] "For the first time, researchers prompted the very rich—people with fortunes in excess of $25 million—to speak candidly about their lives. The result is a surprising litany of anxieties: their sense of isolation, their worries about work and love, and most of all, their fears for their children." Most of the study involved open-ended questions and prompted a response designed to help others understand the fears of this population segment.

Paul G. Schervish, the lead sociologist on the Boston College study, says he likes to quote Deuteronomy: "Behold, I set before you this day a blessing and a curse." As he explains, "Money is like fire: it will warm your feet or it will burn your socks off."[3] However, the positives get most of the press. What I want to do is spend some time highlighting the lesser-known aspects of affluence.

I want to focus on money's power to move our hearts. This kind of change shows up at the deepest level, at the core of who we really are.

## GETTING PERSPECTIVE

No matter what your family of origin or present or future financial status, this book is intended to help you gain a thoughtful perspective for navigating whatever affluence you have.

So many of our choices about money are made in the moment. Our attitudes about spending, though deep-seated, spring up as if from nowhere and cause guilt, anger, frustration, or even despair. We encounter the effects of affluence every day, usually several times a day. Yet few of us have given extended thought to how we approach affluence and to how we want those closest to us (family members and colleagues in particular) to approach affluence.

An important step each of us can take is getting perspective on money. This isn't simply a matter of assenting to a few simple guidelines. It's about really reflecting on how money and your heart are connected. It's about using the questions and examples in these pages to live a life of significance: to matter at what matters.

But what does matter? As I mentioned above, a lot of times we determine what matters in the moment, without taking a longer view. The daily flurry of life can make small decisions seem urgent and important. And they may be! But even these small decisions are best made in light of a grander sense of what is significant. When we simply bounce from conversation to conversation and purchase to purchase, the big picture concerns of life fall by the wayside.

On top of this, affluence changes many dynamics of our personal, social, and business lives. Money makes everything crash harder and bigger. This is true whether we jump into assets quickly (think of a college athlete making the big leagues) or over time (the real estate agent who climbs the ranks in her company for three decades and is now catering to high-end clients).

In order to navigate the flip sides of affluence, we need to have a firm grasp on what matters. My way of talking about what matters is the eternal perspective or, put simply, your legacy. When I talk about legacy, I'm talking about where all of this is headed. I'm talking about not just what I want or see or care about today, but what I will want or see or care about in ten years, or twenty, or fifty or yes, even into eternity.

Getting perspective on affluence means keeping your head up as you navigate financial waters. It's the same principle that holds true when you learn to ride a bike. If you keep focusing on the pedals and your feet, you are in great danger of crashing, and crashing hard. But if you look ahead—at where you are going—the pedals and feet take care of themselves.

When you focus on the destination, you are much more

likely to get there. When you focus on the moment, you may arrive at a destination that is nothing like the one you always wanted.

## A SEAWORTHY LEGACY

What if our legacy was truly seaworthy? What if it could take on an ocean? This type of legacy requires taking the long view. You may already be doing this in some areas of life. But this book is specifically designed to help you do so with respect to money.

Leaving a "seaworthy legacy" means asking not just how far you can go but whether you are going in the right direction. It means coordinating your talents, influence, affluence, and energy toward goals that matter. It means responding to the present in light of where you want to go in the long run.

Let me give you a few examples from my own life. For me, living with this view means responding to a 3 a.m. "Daddy, I wet the bed" moment with grace and encouragement, not frustration. It means sometimes taking a short-term business loss in exchange for a long-term win. It means living in a way that gives me good stories to tell my future grandkids. It means preserving enough energy to listen to my spouse after a long day at work. It means striving to matter where it counts and being engaged and ready day in and day out.

I often need reminders to build a seaworthy legacy; all too often, I raise my voice and do stupid things. But I find I do them less when I keep these thoughts at the top of my mind.

The great football coach Vince Lombardi would start the

season with a lecture that began: "This is a football." Then he would outline how it bounces, how to hold it, and all the things that you would think anyone would know just from looking at it. This was done not just with the rookies, but also with the veterans. Legendary basketball coach John Wooden is only slightly less famous for teaching his players how to put on socks. In his view, putting on your socks wrong could lead to blisters, and blisters meant failing to play at the top of your game.

What both coaches were pointing out is that the basics are crucial. What are the basics in life? What are the core essentials for you? How we live out these basic and core items will form our legacy.

To begin, I'd like you to think not about the future, but about the past. What is your family's legacy? Think for a second about your parents and grandparents. Try to come up with just the first names of your great-grandparents or even their parents. How far back can you go? If you are like most of us, you can get to great-grandparents . . . maybe.

Now, how many stories can you name from those generations of grandparents? My guess is that not many stories will come to mind from those generations. Why is that? And is that what you want to be said of you?

Our legacy story is a way to show our values and identity. Author Donald Miller says, "A story is based on what people think is important, so when we live a story, we are telling people around us what we think is important." Why not live in such a way to create and tell stories that will honor and value your family? Maybe this will even form a collective identity for your family. This book will help you create at least parts of your family story on purpose.

## REMEMBERING WHAT'S IMPORTANT

I find I need to be constantly called back to the important. Don't you? We have a desire to matter, but it is so easy to lose sight of what matters.

For me, the words of the old hymn "Come Thou Fount" ring all too true: "Prone to wander, Lord, I feel it, Prone to leave the God I love." I am prone to get off track with what matters and leave the commitments I hold dear. I need to get back on track.

For me, getting back on track involves Bible reading, prayer, time with family, reading good books, and talking with mentors and friends. It also means setting aside time for true legacy thinking.

I've found few things get me thinking about what matters more than this poignant poem by W. Livingston Larned. But it is slightly dated, so allow me to share it in a newer light.

## DADDY FORGETS

A modernization of Father Forgets by W. Livingston Larned

> Son, I watch you now as you sprawl in your bed, slightly snoring as you breathe. Your hair tousled and wild, a little chalk still on your cheek. I snuck into your room tonight to watch you sleep. As I sat in my chair watching TV, guilt and remorse swept over me. So I came into your room by your bedside.
>
> I know I've been quick with my temper lately, yelling too fast and understanding too little. I yelled at you for forgetting your chores. I

## THE DIFFERENCE MONEY MAKES

was cross because you did not brush your teeth and took you to task for asking me for the required signature on your homework. I was harsh when you didn't clean your room, and had books and Legos spread over the floor and I just stepped on the sharp edge of a wing.

I found fault in how you ate your breakfast, how you wouldn't stay in your seat and "be a man." As you gulped down your food I chastised you for not tasting it—the good food I paid money for. I questioned you about your day like I was the police, not a daddy. When you ran off to school you still shouted, "I love you Daddy!" I merely waved in response.

Again on your way home from school with your friends you were talking about your teacher and what you did at recess. But I broke in and told you to zip up your backpack and start with your chores. Later you began to play football in the mud in the backyard. And I was frustrated you would make a mess and track it all over the house. You began to fuss and I barked an order to march upstairs and clean up. Imagine that from a daddy!

So after dinner while I was watching my show you asked to talk to me and I said, "Not right now, I'm busy." Was I really too busy for my son! But you ran to me and hugged me awkwardly, as I didn't turn towards you. I snapped, "I told you I was busy." Your shoulders dropped as you left the room and I realized then I had gone too far, but I sat there watching you walk away.

Well, kiddo, I sat there for a long time and thought. What have I been doing? I've been finding fault and pointing out only the bad. It's not that I'm not proud of you or that I don't love you. But I was demanding too much of you. I don't have many shades of gray or a good understanding of the stages from toddler to adult. But you are a boy. I was asking and rating you as if you were a man. Evaluating you by the strength of my years.

You have so much about you to praise. You character is strong, and your heart is kind. When you dream it's as though the world in your mind is reality—your imagination really has no bounds. You showed your love for me with that hug but I pushed you away. So I see now I've been foolish. I now am guilt ridden and ashamed of my actions.

I will make things right. I know this wouldn't be clear to you if I spoke this while you were awake so that is why I came into your room to tell you as you slept. Tomorrow I will be a real daddy! I will play with you, laugh and giggle with you. I will hold back my criticism and show patience. I will keep on the top of my mind the saying, "You are but a boy. Just a small boy."

I have seen you as a man, but lying now your legs mixed with the sheets on your bed, I see you as a boy. It seems like yesterday you were crying, newly born, all covered in red …you were beautiful and so tiny.

Yesterday I swaddled you and fed you with a plastic spoon. But today, I have asked too much, too much.

---

**IF YOU HAVEN'T READ THE ORIGINAL "FATHER FORGETS", IT IS EVEN MORE POWERFUL TO READ IN YOUR KID'S ROOM WHILE THEY ARE SLEEPING.**

---

Next chapter, we'll run through some myths about affluence. We'll explore how money and the heart are connected and why that matters to your life.

Nothing is more successful at pulling us off track from a meaningful legacy than money. Affluence pulls us away from mattering at what matters like nothing else.

There's no doubt that money makes a difference. The question is, what difference is it going to make for *you*?

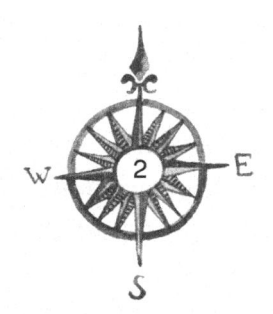

## MONEY AND YOUR HEART

*"Without a rich heart, wealth is an ugly beggar."*
- Ralph Waldo Emerson -

*"Money is the barometer of a society's virtue."*
- Ayn Rand -

*"If a person gets his attitude toward money straight, it will help straighten out almost every other area in his life."*
- Billy Graham -

I remain convinced that money and the heart are intimately connected. Money acts as an amplifier of what is in our heart. It was Jesus who said, "For where your treasure is, there your heart will be also" (Matthew 6:21).

It's amazing to me how investing in a company can make my heart flutter to numbers on a stock ticker. But what deeper effect does it have on my heart? What happens to the heart if I have more than enough money? How does accumulating money create a burden of responsibility? Why does wealth tend to isolate people?

For me, these questions reflect my struggles, both personally and professionally. I've discovered the other side to having more than enough. I've seen a sinister side to affluence. It's amazing to me how quickly and secretively money can grab my heart. Greed, selfishness, hardened hearts, judgment, loneliness, discontentment, separation from others, and relational strife are quite common among those who have more than enough resources.

And I think I'm not the only one who has seen this. Let's look at the extremely affluent from the past and gather their perspectives:

Andrew Carnegie: *"Millionaires seldom smile. Millionaires who laugh are rare. My experience is that wealth is apt to take the smiles away."* Carnegie sold his company in 1901 for $480 million or an equivalent sum today of around $310 billion.

John D. Rockefeller: *"I have made millions, but they have brought me no happiness. I would barter them all for the days I sat on an office stool in Cleveland and counted myself rich on three dollars a week."* Rockefeller is one of the wealthiest people to have walked the earth. His inflation-adjusted net worth in today's dollars has been estimated at $340–660 billion.

John Jacob Astor: *"I am the most miserable man on earth."* Astor was the founding member of the first multi-millionaire family in America. In 1948, he was the wealthiest man alive.

Solomon, King of Israel: *"Whoever loves money never has money enough; whoever loves wealth is never satisfied with his income. This too is meaningless."* His gold mines produced annually over $760 million in today's dollars.

Henry Ford: *"I was happier when doing a mechanic's job."* Ford made Detroit into motor city by transforming factories with the assembly line. His net worth was likely equal to around $199 billion in today's money.

Despite these statements by prominent people of wealth, most Americans' hopes are best summed up by this quote from comedian Spike Milligan: "All I ask is the chance to prove that money can't make me happy." Even though we've heard about the downsides, we're willing to take the risk, perhaps thinking that, for us, things will be different. We hope to enjoy the upsides but avoid the downsides.

When you think of very affluent people—more affluent than you—does your heart fill with envy or with some weird form of emotion you don't fully grasp? When you hear about the downsides of money, do you have the attitude, "Poor rich guys, it must be nice to have their problems"? Isn't it easy to think of their problems as different from ours or mine, even if you earn a good salary or have a fair amount of savings in the bank?

For those who remain unconvinced about the slippery beast of money grabbing hold of your heart, let me offer a short quiz. Be honest and take your time on each question. I've found them personally very challenging—some of them too challenging at times. We will be discussing many of these questions in the chapters that follow.

1. Do you eat differently on a cruise or a buffet than a place with à la carte dining?

2. Does the idea of giving all your money to your kids today create anxiety?

3. Are you motivated by a free sample or gift?

4. Have you ever bought something because it's on sale even though you didn't need it?

5. Do you ever fear being taken advantage of financially?

6. Do you choose vacation spots and time off based primarily on how much it costs? (Did you object strongly in your head to the last question saying, "Well... who doesn't choose a vacation based on money, buddy?")

7. Do you hide the costs of certain items from close friends out of concern over their reactions?

8. Have you ever quantified how much money is enough money to maintain your current lifestyle and/or to plan for your desired lifestyle in retirement?

9. Have you ever put a number on how much you should spend each month?

10. When is the last time you delayed a purchase that wasn't needed?

Let's take a moment to look back at this short quiz. Here are the general themes I see with my friends and clients. See if they are your themes, too:

- The wealthy feel guilt, and sometimes even shame, about their assets.

- Nobody thinks they are truly wealthy because they all know someone who makes more or has more.

- No one really wants to budget.

- The wealthy have a huge fear about asset protection.

- Money doesn't guarantee security because we rarely ask how much is enough.
- The wealthy think they are never doing enough at work and never doing enough at home either—they feel like there is not enough of them to go around.
- Most people have no clue, really, how much they are spending.
- Having wealth doesn't take away things like fights about money.

Many of us have issues with money. Some of us focus way too much time and energy on the numbers, the investment accounts, the net worth statements, and our cash flow. Others are largely ignorant of their own assets, choosing to turn a blind eye to the details for fear of what they might find there.

The funny thing is, no matter what our experiences with money, most of us struggle alone. Most of us don't really talk to anyone else about our thoughts or feelings about wealth. So why is the topic of money so charged? Why can't we talk about it? If I were to disclose my net worth to you, would that change our relationship? If I were to share my income, would you think that was inappropriate?

Because talking about money seems to be taboo in many settings, we suffer in silence with greed, fear, and anxiety. We don't talk about it. Maybe we have the same conversations over and over again in our head. One of my main aims in this book is to get the discussion started, and to make money something that you don't have to face alone.

When we go through these issues for the most part alone, the issues go unnamed, unchallenged, and unchecked.

Many of us have misconceptions about what money does and does not do. Let's cover some of the initial issues up front. As you walk through this list, consider how these misconceptions have influenced you or others who are close to you.

## COMMON MISCONCEPTIONS ABOUT MONEY AND AFFLUENCE

### *Myth #1: If I had more money, I would act differently than I do now.*

We tend to think that if we made more, we would save more. In reality, this is unlikely.

Have you ever heard of the frog in the pot analogy? A frog dropped in a pot of boiling water will try to jump out. But a frog put in cold water and slowly brought to a boil will stay in until it's too late. So, if you increase in wealth little by little, chances are your expenses will increase too.

If you are up to your eyeballs in debt on $4,000 a month of income (the average American's income and debt situation), you'll most likely just have more significant debt if you get to $40,000 a month of income. The best indicator of future financial success is your current situation. There is no reason to think that your money-related behavior will change just because you earn or inherit more money.

### *Myth #2: If I had more money, I'd be more generous in my giving while spending about the same.*

Do you think you would give more if you had more? This may be true, but the stats aren't in your favor. Research shows that, percentage-wise, the more people make, the smaller percentage of their income they give. Statistically, those who make between $45,000 and $50,000 give 4% of their income. Yet those making between $200,000 and $250,000 give only 2.4%. This trend does slightly reverse when income rises above $250,000 to look like an inverse "U." Yet giving by percent (outside of those on the very top, making over $10M) is highest among those earning the least.[4]

---

YOU ARE LIVING ON A PERCENT OF YOUR TOTAL INCOME NOW. I BET YOU DON'T KNOW WHAT PERCENT IT IS. WHY NOT GO GRAB YOUR TAX RETURN AND SEE WHAT PERCENT YOU ARE LIVING ON. YOU MAY BE SURPRISED.

---

Parkinson's law states, "Work expands so as to fill the time available for its completion." Here's how it plays out financially: "As income rises, expenses rise."

The truth is, spending money is an appetite that grows the more we feed it. I agree with Thomas Fuller, who said, "Riches enlarge rather than satisfy appetites." The problem with spending is that the more you spend, the more you will want to spend. There is no final purchase to end the desire to spend, just like there is no meal to end all meals. Spending can creep amazingly silently into places you didn't plan. I'm sure you can give an example or two here. It starts out small, like buying slightly more expensive wine or a higher quality shirt. Then that one nice shirt makes the other shirts you own feel cheap, so you enter a new shirt level. Then there will be one event where you feel the need to upgrade the shoes, since "the shirt never really went with cheap shoes anyway." Then, soon enough, you'll find you call yourself "a bit of a shoe girl." Or maybe you will be "a bit of a car guy" or "sort of a watch person" or "a bit of a purse gal." I've heard the same phrase uttered so many times to justify purchase upgrades in certain areas. Notice that we rarely say, "I'm an aficionado," because we know someone else who is really an aficionado.

Once you enter the new level, going back is not easy.

### *Myth #3: Having more money will make my problems go away.*

Yes and no. Certain problems may go away when you have more money. But other problems will multiply. For instance, you may face more complexity concerning taxation, investments, estate planning, and family and other relationships, to name a few. As Groucho Marx said, "While money can't buy happiness, it certainly lets you choose your own form of misery." While you may have more choice, you will not be problem-free.

Money is an amplifier of life. The problems you struggle with without money will be the same ones you struggle with later. But the increasing zeroes add to the pressure. If you have more money and you still aren't happy, you are failing to live up to your own expectations or the expectations you think others have of you. The acquisition of money can be as much of a burden as a boon.

To push this a little further, think back on your last pay increase. Did your rise in income increase or decrease your pressure? Did it specifically solve any problems? Did it create more, especially concerning your self-perception or relationships with others? Most people find that an increase in money increases stress and sometimes even multiplies difficulty. But we often think too simplistically about solutions to our problems. And, as mentioned above, we typically deal with money issues all alone. So there is little push back on any aberrant idea, and it's easy to convince ourselves that money holds all the answers. When we put the blame on someone or something else for our problems, we don't have to face our issues head-on. We simply defer dealing with them until later.

---

> "NEARLY ALL MEN CAN STAND THE TEST OF ADVERSITY, BUT IF YOU REALLY WANT TO TEST A MAN'S CHARACTER, GIVE HIM POWER."
> **- ABRAHAM LINCOLN -**

---

## *Myth #4: Just a little bit more is enough.*

Take a second to consider: How much money do you need in order to reach your goals? The simple answer is, more. But how much more? Is just a little more enough?

We erroneously think we are dissatisfied currently because we don't have that one new thing. But have the increases in your wealth thus far made you more satisfied with your possessions? If you are typical, the increase in wealth will have increased your appetite, not your satisfaction. More money really serves to make you more aware of the amazing, and often expensive, things you were not even conscious you could spend money on!

Famously John D. Rockefeller was asked, "How much is enough?" His response? "Just a little bit more." You may have heard that before, but did you know he said that at a time when his net worth at its height was a 1.5-2% of the national GDP?[5]

Since there is never enough, we act as though there is never enough. We drive and push for more. Ambition can be good, but what really causes you to drive so hard? Is your drive always healthy? Or has it potentially, at times, come from unhealthy desires or been expressed in an unhealthy manner? Are you honest enough with yourself to actually see a season of your life when you were not operating under a healthy ambition?

### *Myth #5: I'd feel secure if I had more money, or money provides security.*

If money in and of itself provided security, the wealthy would not spend so much time worrying over it, focusing on it, and protecting it. Security doesn't come from money alone; there is never enough money to make us feel secure, since our lifestyles grow with our incomes. When spending and lifestyle are near or even above income, there will always be fighting and struggle. Unchecked desires, expanded lifestyle spending, and monthly bills without margin put great pressure on marriages, families, and individuals.

Security concerns grow with the size of your net worth. In

a 2007 Prince and Associates study, among those with a net worth from $500-$1 million, only 17.6% feared being sued. But among those with a net worth of $20 million, 83.5% feared "being unjustly sued."[6]

It was Pastor William Carl Ketcherside who first said, "Our problem is not the high cost of living but the cost of high living." Now, we think, I need to make $XYZ income just to stay the same. Have you ever met a driven, high-achieving individual who likes to be stagnant? Are you okay being stagnant? Unless you can answer an unequivocal "yes," you will not find that money provides security.

### *Myth #6: Money provides happiness and contentment.*

Contrary to most of our expectations, contentment doesn't come from money. Pastor Chip Ingram has it right when he says, "Contentment is a learned attitude." More money often leads the affluent into discontentment, not contentment.

The big lie here is that standard of living equals quality of life. But really, these two are not directly connected. If they were, then those with the highest incomes would be the happiest and have the best quality of life. Is that true? If you need to be convinced, re-read the quotes at the beginning of the chapter.

More money may equal more choices, but after a certain point, having more choices leads us away from, not toward, contentment and peace of mind. Peter Huizenga, by any measure, is a successful businessman. From his early days of being one of the first officers of Waste Management to now running a hedge fund, he has stayed fully engaged with business.

Describing his experience, Huizenga says, "There's an indescribable urge to think that money provides happiness and joy, an emotional high. But it's temporary—fleeting."

According to Malcolm Gladwell's book *David and Goliath*, psychologist James Grubman argues that happiness decreases once you reach income over $75,000. And a recent CNN/ORC International poll, conducted from May 29 to June 1, 2014, found that "most people know in their hearts that … money can't guarantee true happiness." That dovetails with a 2010 Princeton study that found emotional wellbeing rose with income, but not much beyond an annual income of $75,000.

To see an indicator of this, look at the changes in luxury cars over the last few decades. What were considered luxury features in the 1990s versus today? When did power windows become standard, not optional? When did every car need a GPS? How about heated seats (even in the south)? Or, now, air-conditioned seats and auto-driving cars, right? I'm not against nice cars or new inventions. But why are we letting marketing ploys and envy drive our view of need? How have our expectations about a "nice" versus a "basic" or "adequate" car changed, and why?

What was yesterday's luxury often becomes today's need.

### *Myth #7: We'd fight less about money if we had more.*

Money isn't what we fight about; it's the quantifiable arena where we fight. We fight about priorities, time, and opinions. Money allows us to quantify and fund our desires. Those desires are still there when you have more money.

More money won't solve ambition and priority issues. They will keep creeping into our fights and actions no matter how much money we earn.

I've found the problems and fights we have are the same with or without money. But the more money we have, the more pressure surrounds the fights. The disagreements stay the same, but the arguments may become more heated.

The stress of being rich is odd. This is true of the affluence associated with position or job, as well as with cash in the bank. There is often a pressure that comes with money that is hard to describe to those who don't have it. Bosses and owners, despite their apparent richness of title or wealth, often lose sleep over the stresses of the job. Whether it's the need to pay salaries during a down season or the challenge of keeping growth happening, there is a unique burden that those in the lead must shoulder. And when you share this pressure, it's common to be accused of being overly focused on the bottom line or of being someone who always talks about or only cares about money.

I remember discussing this pressure with one man who said, "I am misunderstood at work. But I'm okay with it. I go into my shell and ignore the ones I can't impact. I have sort of figured I can't win them all [to my viewpoint]." This may be the best response he has to a difficult situation. But do you hear how that man could be lonely?

### *Myth #8: The grass is greener on the other side.*

There is not better than here. It's just different. The problem is, we know the warts of life here, and we see the highlight reel of life there. We simply don't have all the info on their life. We are comparing all we know about us to the little we know about them. That's not fair.

As a Midwest boy, I remember those fields we'd drive by that smelled up to high heaven. In other words, if the grass was greener, it was usually because the fertilizer (the manure) was stronger.

The Boston College study on the "Super Rich" again shared something insightful. The survey respondents shared that they have "lost the right to complain about anything, for fear of sounding—or being—ungrateful." This applies even to family loss and death. Shockingly, one respondent shared the feeling that a death in the family was not viewed as a "real problem" by several whom she thought were friends. Even in tragedy, the wealthy seem to be not able to share and express their felt level of pain with those who are not wealthy.[7] This suggests that, among other things, the grass may not be so much greener but simply hiding deeper uncertainties, pain, or loneliness.

## OVERARCHING THEMES

The overarching theme that runs through all of these myths and their corresponding realities is that yes, money or affluence may allow you to pick your battles, but it doesn't eliminate the struggle, difficulty, trials, and pain that are a part of every life. One man I interviewed said it succinctly: "The biggest problems in life we share are the same, whether we're affluent or not." Relational pain is there at any income level. Your children can cause joy and pain equally without regard to your net worth. Money pulls on your heart no matter how much you do or don't have.

You can't buy your way out of life's problems. In fact, the bottom line is that many of our misconceptions about money originate with our own sense of unhappiness or with our sense that someone else is to blame. We act as though we are not responsible for our own perceptions and attitudes. But are we? Is more money the best answer, or are there issues that we could address now, at our current or even a lesser income level?

The way we evaluate wealth is largely relative to others in our immediate circles. As you read this book, do you think you're wealthy or affluent? In someone else's eyes, you might be. Think about the history of the world and some of the amenities we have that the elite of the past never enjoyed. We have more variety in our options, diet, travel, and entertainment than ever before. We are indeed well-off, given our libraries and access to information alone—and think of recent advances in health care, technology, and transportation! The list can go on.

Regardless of where you stand with respect to wealth, it's important to take a closer look at your hopes and dreams concerning future dollars. My advice is to dream about these matters in light of eternity—to take the long view.

## LEGACY THINKING

Success is great. But it needs to lead into significance. I love the John Maxwell saying, "Success is when I add value to myself. Significance is when I add value to others."

Our success needs to be the right kind. In his book *Crazy Love*, Francis Chan says, "Our greatest fear should not be of failure but of succeeding at things in life that don't matter."[8] (Take down your cat poster and put that quote on your wall instead.) I never want to win at work but lose my family. That, to me, is a bad day. My aim is for success to be well-rounded. I want to seize my wife's heart, not only to prevail at work. I want my little daughters to run into my arms when I walk in the door. I want my boys to want to spend time with me. Success is not only about larger accounts, a bigger house, and more influence at work.

Dwight Eisenhower's quote proves very true in this dilemma: "Most things which are urgent are not important, and most things which are important are not urgent." We need to keep the focus on the important matters of life in order to ensure we are mattering. What does that include for you?

For me, that includes my faith, my family, and all of my relationships. I think God designed you and me to make an impact. In Genesis, God commands Adam to go subdue the earth. How's that for a huge task? The actual words are "... God blessed them. And God said to them, 'Be fruitful and multiply and fill the earth and subdue it, and have dominion over the fish of the sea and over the birds of the heavens and over every living thing that moves on the earth'" (Genesis 1: 28, ESV). That is a call to work, to contribute, and to go big—really big.

Unfortunately, money is often the largest deterrent keeping us off the path we truly desire, the path to building a seaworthy legacy that will weather all of life's storms and offer lasting significance.

## LEGACY FORMATION

A seaworthy legacy requires purposed steps toward being significant and mattering at what really matters. For me, true purpose comes from a Christian worldview and is driven by the gospel. My legacy is formed in light of a moment like the final verse of the old hymn "Amazing Grace." If you remember the words of the fourth verse ("…when we've been there 10,000 years, bright shining as the sun…"), that heavenly moment is what I live for today.

If I live in light of that heavenly moment, I think my decisions today make much more sense. In my marriage, if I'm living for today, I won't really take time to woo my wife. But if I live in light of the gleam in her eye I want to see at our sixtieth wedding anniversary, I need to act differently now.

If I live my life in light of building the tree fort with my grandkids or walking my daughter down the aisle, my decisions today are better. If I imagine bouncing my grandkids on my knees, I make better parenting decisions now. If, in business, I work on growing my company in light of what I want others to say about it in the Wall Street Journal in 30 years, I will make better decisions rather than focusing only on this quarter's returns.

But a list of goals is not motivational. It's not emotional. For goals to move you to change, they need to reach the spot of emotions. You need to connect emotionally with your legacy story. You may or may not share my Christian faith, or perhaps you once did but have now lost faith in God or the Church (if so, consider reading Appendix A of this book). But whether you are a person of Christian faith, another faith, or none at all, I encourage you to consider how long-term thinking can shape your legacy formation. Remembering and revisiting your own legacy story is crucial to shaping your own legacy both now and over time.

## EVALUATION

At the end of each chapter, I'll give you some questions to consider. I know that when I read books and they tell me to do something, I usually skip it. But try this one. This chapter has likely stirred up some reactions in you. Take a moment to write those down.

Until you have to actually define your ideas and thoughts—pen in hand—they will not be fully formed. There is something so beautiful about seeing your thoughts in written form. United States senator S. I. Hayakawa once said, "You don't know anything clearly unless you can state it in writing."

Write something about these questions:

1. What is the reason you are as affluent as you are? Really wrestle with this one. Contest mightily with your soul on this. What could be the reason you are as blessed as you are? As gifted as you are? As connected as you are? As rich as you are? What is the reason you have been entrusted with much?

2. As we've been talking through this idea around legacy, and mattering at what matters, what purpose are you living for? What thoughts have been brewing in the back of your mind about this? What would your ideal legacy story look like?

If you haven't written anything down yet, now is the time. I've found that my answers sometimes change once I start writing.

Instead of rushing ahead to check a box, take a few moments to reflect on and revise your thoughts if you need to.

3. What matters most to you? Alfred Adler notes, "Simply asking yourself what you are living for is not a useful endeavor." Instead, a better way to answer what we are living for is to look at our fears and nightmares. He says your deepest emotions—anxiety, fear, or despair—will point you to your god.

What we fear will show us what matters to us. And don't just say, my kids' future makes me pause. What about their future? Is it your child being a trust fund baby who doesn't work? Is it them getting into drugs or other addictions? It is that your money will define them?

Next, we'll dive into how we get sidetracked from being significant at what matters, discuss why success can feel empty, look at a more helpful view of winning and success, and walk through some internal objections that keep us living by default rather than by purposed design.

**Suggested Reading**
*Treasure Principle* by Randy Alcorn
*Wealth Conundrum* by Ralph Doudera
*To Whom Much Is Given* by Jay Link

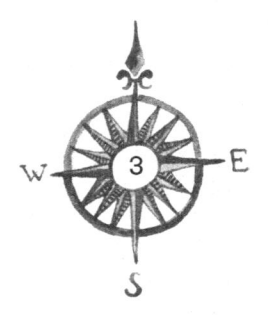

# SUCCESS, ACHIEVEMENT, AND SIGNIFICANCE

*"Our greatest fear should not be of failure but of succeeding at things in life that don't really matter."*
- Francis Chan -

*"Make no little plans; they have no magic to stir men's blood and probably themselves will not be realized."*
- Daniel Burnham -

*"This is mankind's age-old dilemma in the face of death: What man really fears is not so much extinction, but extinction with insignificance. Man wants to know that his life has somehow counted, that it has left a trace, a trace that has meaning. And in order for anything once alive to have meaning, its effect must remain alive in eternity some way."*
- Ernest Becker -

In the movie *The Emperor's Club*, Kevin Kline plays a Western Civilization teacher. Above his classroom door is a quote:

I am Shutruk Nahunte, King of Ashand and Susa, Sovereign of the Land of Elam. By the Command of Inshushinak, I destroyed Sippar, took the Stele of Nirah-Sin, and brought it back to Elam, where I erected it as an offering to my God, Inshushinak.

**– Shutruk Nahunte, 1158 B.C.**

In one scene, the teacher asks the class,

Is anyone familiar with this fellow? Texts are permissible, but you won't find him there. Shutruk Nahunte. King. Sovereign of Elam. Destroyer of Sippar. But behold his accomplishments cannot be found in any history book. Why?—Because great ambition and conquest without contribution are without significance.

There's something right about that last line: "Great ambition and conquest without contribution are without significance." We all want to matter. We all want to be significant. Although it seems strange, pursuing success can actually get in the way of significance.

How we define success determines how we pursue it. Many people achieve what they once thought was success, but are left feeling defeated and unfulfilled. The finish line looks different after they've arrived.

Some of us operate with multiple competing ideas of what success really is, making it difficult to tell whether we've prioritized the right things or whether we've achieved success. Oftentimes we view success like a dog chasing a car; we don't really think through what happens if we catch it.

This chapter presents an opportunity for you to think about success, achievement, and significance, perhaps in new ways that will help you sort through what really matters in life. To say it bluntly, I'm not trying to talk you out of life in the fast lane; I'm trying to make sure you're on the right road.

Your contribution is not the same thing as your success. Remember the John Maxwell quote from the last chapter: "Success is when I add value to myself. Significance is when I add value to others."[9] Adding value to others is your contribution. That is what leads to significance.

Contribution is not limited to the workplace. It involves your whole life: the relationships you build, the people you help, the conversations you start, the problems you solve, the beauty you create.

What I've come to believe is that success without contribution is success without significance. In fact, maybe it isn't even success at all. One example of this is the life of Wayne Huizenga, Jr.

In full disclosure: Wayne is family. He was part of that great chorus of extended family members that sang "win zijn familie" ("we are family") on our family trip to the Netherlands a few decades ago.

Wayne's story exemplifies perfectly the difference between the life of a "Shutruk Nahante" and a life of significance. Wayne Jr. started his career as a clerk in his father's company, a start-up in Miami called Blockbuster Video. He excelled at his job and was constantly moving up the ranks. Before long, he was responsible for management of Huizenga's Holdings. This group, run by Wayne Sr., at one point claimed ownership of the Miami Dolphins (NFL), the Florida Marlins (MLB), and the Florida Panthers (NHL). Today, Wayne Jr. runs a superyacht refit company called Rybovich in southern Florida. From the outside, Wayne Jr.'s success looked like the American dream. He had money, prestige, position in a growing company, and all the glory to go with it. He had all the trappings of success. Yet he still seemed unfulfilled. In a recent conversation, he described his life like sitting down at Thanksgiving feast expecting to be more than satisfied, but then walking away feeling unfulfilled. What should have left him full left him hungering for something more. As Wayne put it, "I was happy, but I was never fully satisfied."

If you want to hear Wayne's story in his own words, take a look at his interview on the website "I am Second." What he basically says is this: there was something about professional success that just didn't fulfill him. Achievement, promotion, money, prestige . . . none of these were enough.[10]

Wayne Jr. is not the only successful person to express a deeper angst that isn't addressed by acquisition or wealth. Renee Lockey shares a similar sentiment after completing her doctorate and residency in Obstetrics and Gynecology. She said, "I had accomplished everything I set out to accomplish. I had a successful career. I was out of debt. But I hit a point when realized I had all this, but was not in the content place I thought I'd be. It was an uncomfortable place to be in to realize that I had accomplished my goals, but now what? There was an emptiness inside, as if something was missing."[11]

Tom Brady, a future Hall of Fame quarterback with the New England Patriots, said something similar after he won three Super Bowl rings in the span of four years. "Why do I have three Super Bowl rings and still think there's something greater out there for me? I mean, maybe a lot of people would say, 'Hey man, this is what is.' I reached my goal, my dream, my life. I think, 'God, it's got to be more than this.' I mean this isn't, this can't be what it's all cracked up to be."[12]

Ted Turner, who launched CNN as the first 24-hour news channel and, in the process, made a few billion dollars, shared a similar sentiment in an interview with Barbara Walters. She asked, "Ted, with all your success, are you happy?" Turner's response, without hesitation, was "Success is an empty bag, but you don't know it until you achieve it." Success, an empty bag? Here was one man at the pinnacle of success, yet obviously still searching for happiness.

Allow me to share just one more case study, and perhaps you can think of others, too. Janice Worth made her fortune as an entrepreneur in the spa business. However, having been orphaned at a young age, she viewed money as a pathway to security, a safety net. Janice admits that she has always loved money—making it, spending it, and giving it away. Yet even in the peak of her financial success, she shares, her life was empty for years. "It's far worse to feel alone with someone than alone by yourself."[13]

For Janice and many others like her, success got in the way of her ability to matter at what matters. She arrived at a point where she felt stuck and alone and was searching for answers. There was a hole right in the middle of her success.

In all five of these case studies, we see that success and money provide ample obstacles to significance. Why is this true? What about success left these individuals feeling like there is something missing? After all, aren't we all taught from a very early age to aim for success?

I can think of at least two good answers to these questions. The first is that there's more to life than living in the moment and achieving success from day to day. That is, there's something bigger and grander than life lived on a human scale. I don't know what your thoughts on religion might be, but I believe that each of us has an eternal soul and that what we do during our lives actually matters for the life beyond. This is part of why I emphasize an eternal viewpoint—because I think that seeing the "big picture" can help us make sense of the "little picture" or day-to-day ups and downs.

Another good answer is this: we're often taught what to aim at but not how to aim at it. We know that winning is good. We know that promotions and pay raises are good. We know that getting recognized by peers or colleagues is good. You could probably jot down ten things on the spot that most, if not all, people would classify as "good."

We know the endgame. But do we know how to play the game? For instance, think back to your early life. Were you taught not only to make good grades, but also to have a healthy approach to achievement and failure? Were you taught not only to push yourself on the athletic field so that you could set records and win championships, but also to balance activity with rest and to pay attention to what kind of food you put into your body? Were you taught that making a good salary is a great goal, but not the only worthy goal? That how you make money might matter just as much as what you make?

In what follows, we will take a step back and ask ourselves, what does it mean to be successful? How are success and significance related? Does one automatically lead to the other? And what do we need to pay attention to in order to pursue both?

## WINNING AT THE RIGHT THING

The desire for success seems to be hardwired into so many of us. We all want to win. I want to win. And I don't want to change that. But let's look at how we define a win.

We often think of success as reaching a certain point of accomplishment. Lawyers dream of the day they complete law school. Doctors count the days until they finish medical school or residency. Mothers-to-be look forward to their delivery date. Along the way, we build up expectations about what life will be like on the other side of those goals.

We think things will feel a certain way after we succeed. But so many of us find that what we thought was the pinnacle of success turns out to be just one more step in the journey. We're pressing toward a goal, but that goal doesn't turn out to be the end point, or even to be as rewarding as we thought it would be. We long to be a millionaire; then we see those zeros in our account, and it doesn't feel like we thought it would. Perhaps you can think of a situation in your own life when you felt like this. You thought you arrived, but that wasn't the end of it.

Another thing that happens is that one goal immediately replaces another. We finish the degree, get the pay raise, earn the promotion, exceed the funding goal, or successfully move our children through all the phases of elementary through high school—even college. But as soon as one box is checked, another one fills in its place. At first we don't really notice this. But after a while we begin to realize perhaps there's no such thing as arriving.

What will happen if we stop looking at success as a destination and instead understand it as a journey? What if we shift our focus from reaching a goal to the process of moving toward that goal?

There are really two elements to this change. I am not saying we should abandon all goals. But I am saying that what we often think are important goals may be less important when viewed in light of the overall significance of our life. Over time, I have shifted from viewing goals as endpoints to viewing goals as markers along the way, that tell me where I am and where I'm going.

Part of the problem with the "arriving" view of success is the byproducts of pride, envy, jealousy, or toxic shame. Either I hit my goal and quickly become all about me (i.e., prideful or even narcissistic), or I miss my goal and am therefore ashamed or loathe myself and envy others. I'm not a big fan of either result. Yet I love goals.

> "THAT WHICH WE OBTAIN TOO EASILY, WE ESTEEM TOO LIGHTLY. IT IS DEARNESS ONLY WHICH GIVES EVERYTHING ITS VALUE." THOMAS PAINE. (THAT IS ANOTHER GOOD POSTER QUOTE, BETTER THAN A CAT POSTER RIGHT THERE).

Maybe we should change our focus from success and work to contribution. When we discuss work or career, we automatically consider making money, but contribution concerns making a difference. Success is typically self-focused, but contribution is focused on making the world better. When we talk about contribution, the retiree, inheritor, and stay-at-home mom can join in the discussion, and that discussion becomes more significant.

## HOW DO WE CHANGE OUR VIEW?

Most of our goals are not seen as part of a bigger idea. We usually live in light of the next three to five days. The next few years are less important, and our lifetime or eternity is least important. What if we flip that paradigm on its head? What if we live as though the next three to five days are the least important, the next years are more important, and the rest of our lives (extending into eternity) is most important? Think of how much that would change our decision-making process!

If our view of success changes, so much else will change. Viewing success as a journey makes it easier to have impact beyond our last breath. We shift from thinking merely of success and begin focusing on succeeding at what matters.

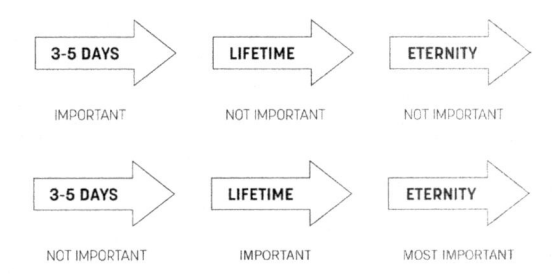

| 3-5 DAYS → | LIFETIME → | ETERNITY → |
|---|---|---|
| IMPORTANT | NOT IMPORTANT | NOT IMPORTANT |

| 3-5 DAYS → | LIFETIME → | ETERNITY → |
|---|---|---|
| NOT IMPORTANT | IMPORTANT | MOST IMPORTANT |

This type of success leads not only to financial success, but also influence within relationships. It's not merely about money, career, promotion, or status. It's about talents, relationships, and long-term impact within your sphere of influence. It's true affluence, not just monetary affluence.

## TALKING POINTS

Here is an exercise to get you started down the right path and to help you uncover the details of your personal passions. Imagine you could have time with the President of the United States, a star athlete, a rising celebrity, or anyone with a high net worth. Or suppose the Bill and Melinda Gates Foundation called you up to ask a few questions about where and how to disperse their grant funds. What would you want to talk about? Where would you want to direct their attention? Take a second to think about it and jot down a few ideas.

Now, think beyond the realm of financial affluence. Let's say you have thirty minutes to say whatever you want to the 400 wealthiest families in America. What are your talking points? What is important for them to know, think about, believe, or do?

You probably have one of two reactions to these questions. Either you know immediately what you would say, or you really have no idea what you would say. Your reaction might have something to do with whether or not you think of yourself as affluent and whether you have reflected on the best use of personal affluence.

No matter which camp you fall into, taking some time to answer these questions in more depth will give you important insight on where you are headed and what you value. Emotions and passion are typically connected. If you are struggling to come up with a list of talking points, notice what makes you mad. When do you feel shame? What personal experiences still have big emotions connected to them? What causes make you most excited, agitated, or upset?

Now I would like you to consider another illuminating question.

## WHY ARE YOU AFFLUENT?

This question relates to both your past and your future. First, it's a question about your personal history. What circumstances, people, decisions, relationships, events, etc., have contributed to your current level of affluence? What is your story? Perhaps you are less affluent now than you used to be. Why is that? What experiences have shaped you into the person you are today?

At the same time, this question also has a future dimension: for what purpose are you affluent? Why do you think you are affluent, or how do you view your responsibilities as a person of affluence? Who are you responsible to (an individual, a segment of society, a group, a family, etc.)?

The final question I have brings both of these exercises together. Let's assume for a moment that the things you wanted to tell other affluent people are the things you really think are important. And let's assume that in thinking about your past and your future, you have identified some key aspects of your personal identity.

Here's the really tough question: how does your advice to

other people connect with your advice for yourself?

Now, to get personal, how many of the issues you wanted to address with them are issues you are currently taking action on? Really, on a day-to-day basis, how many important issues are you making progress on? I would argue our focus is too often on the next few days and not on the long haul—on the big-picture things we think are really important. Forget about what someone else should do for the moment. Focus instead on your own choices and issues. It's too easy to think about these issues in light of someone else's experiences, not our own.

Let's look at some common objections as to why we are not seeing movement on what matters to us.

**Objection #1: But I'm not that affluent.**

A 2011 Gallup poll says that most people don't think they are rich. No matter what they are making right now, most people think that, in order to be rich, they'd have to double their income. Andy Stanley summarizes, "In other words, when they interviewed people who earned $30,000 a year, that group defined 'rich' as someone who earns $60,000. When they interviewed people who earned $50,000 a year, the magic number was $100,000."[14] The more you earn, the more you think you need to earn in order to count as wealthy.

In another study conducted by PNC, the focus was on how much money someone needed in order to feel secure. Robert Frank summarized what the financial group found by saying, "Those worth $500,000 to $1 million said they needed $2.4 million to feel secure. Those worth $1 million to $1.49 million needed $3 million. And those worth $10 million or more said they needed $18 million."[15] So, clearly, feeling rich or secure is not just a matter of having a certain amount of assets. We tend to think of those who have more than us as rich or secure. We wonder what it must be like to spend whatever we'd like, whenever we'd like. But that's certainly not our situation, so we don't think of ourselves as rich.

All of this works together to make us think in at least two categories—us and them. And this makes us want to delay dealing with money matters. "When I earn $100,000 a year, that's when I'll pay attention." "When I earn $200,000, that's when I'll assess my investments." "When I have one million in cash, then I'll reset my priorities." So our thinking goes.

However, our concepts of what it means to be rich are very much conditioned by those around us. When we look outside of North America and consider the global economy, the standard of what it means to be rich changes drastically.

It has become popular in the U.S. lately to refer to "the one-percenters," that is, the top one percent of earners. Popular rhetoric decries the one-percenters as filthy rich or as getting more than their fair share of assets, perhaps by questionable means.

In the U.S., those in the top one percent either earn just over $500,000 a year, or they have over five million dollars in assets.[16] But if we expand our gaze to include the whole world, then anyone earning over $32,000 is a "one-percenter"! This is the finding of www.globalrichlist.com, a site that puts wealth in global perspective. In light of this, almost anyone who is reading this book is likely a one-percenter.

So, what are we to take from this? First, I hope this discussion leads to gratitude and not guilt. These stats are about today's affluence, let alone where we stand in historical wealth and luxury. Let's turn to gratitude and truly be thankful for what we've been given.

Yet you are not jumping up and down with gratitude, are you? Why not? Because wealth and affluence are relative. And we compare our stuff to theirs—whoever "they" is for you. We know all about our situation and very little about them, and we still compare.

Now I'm starting to meddle and push you into some uncomfortable areas. I know. But what if we took this challenge seriously and thought of ourselves as already affluent? What if we thought of ourselves as rich and started to act like it? What if we started to work on those big things we want to push off for someone else to do? What if we stopped looking so much at the next few days and lived instead in light of eternity?

**Objection #2: I can't do it all.**

Changing the way we think about and deal with money can be a daunting task—especially once we begin to see how money permeates so many areas of our lives. How we spend, save, or earn money affects everything from where we live to what we own and how we spend our work time and free time.

So, it's easy to look at the task of making sense of all of this and to say, "I can't do it all. I can't take on a task this monumental. At least not right now!"

Like any half-truth, there's something right about this. You may not be able to change everything at once. You may not even be able to change everything ever! But we are still responsible for what we can change.

Small changes add up over time, even though that's hard to see in the moment. I've heard it said that we tend to overestimate what we can do in a year but underestimate what we can do in five. How many personal projects have you begun and stuck with for up to five years? Thinking long-term can help us see how changes in the short-term really add up.

The key is, you have to start somewhere. Mother Teresa once wisely said, "If you can't feed a hundred people, then feed just one." If you can't change everything, change something.

Let's take a moment to apply this to your personal situation. During the exercise early about the "Talking Points" for the rich, your inner dialogue about money began to emerge. Whatever you said a rich person should do is a clue to what your ideals are—that is, to what you think people should be and do. Our ideals shape our decisions and give us something to aim for.

Why not begin today with making your ideals more of a reality? You can do this without earning one more penny.

**Objection #3: This isn't who I am.**

Somewhere in the process, you may ask this question, "Why me? Why do I have assets?" If you are a Bible reader, go to the story where Moses tries to tell God that he is not the right man for the job (Exodus 4:10 and following). If God has called you for a job, who are you to tell him you are not the one for the calling?

I concur with the famed football coach Lou Holtz, who said,

"I can't believe that God put us on this earth to be ordinary." Why not you? Why not now? Do extraordinary things only you can do, with what only you've been given, in a way only you can, and in the time you still have left! Rather than denying the financial aspects of your identity, make the most of them.

## MOVING FORWARD

We can either live by default or by design. I think we can all agree with Peter Drucker's statement, "Nothing good happens by default." He should know. He's often called the "Father of Modern Management."

I want to challenge you to visualize your purpose. If we are going to make any lasting change, we need to connect with that emotional spot. Our goals need to connect and resonate emotionally, even bringing us to tears.

If this is new thinking, some headings can be helpful to begin to crystalize your thinking. We can place legacies into three categories: love for a person; a passion for a cause; or a spiritual calling. These are somewhat self-explanatory, but I'll highlight each of them briefly.

1. Love for a person. This one is almost universal. We all want to have an impact on the people we love. But how? Do you want to go deep or wide? Which way do you want to turn your rectangle of impact? Flat and wide, impacting many but only in a small way? Or deep impact, yet only with a few people? Does the list include only your immediate family or all people in your occupation? Where are you doing this well and where do you see room for improvement?

2. A passion for a cause. Breast cancer, orphan care, evangelism, education, poverty alleviation, political reform, rare disease, clean water—the list can go on and on. Which ones get you up in the morning? Where does your heartbeat quicken?
3. A spiritual calling. What do you believe about the human spirit or God's Spirit? What would you like other people to know about their significance in life? What will your role be in sharing your convictions about spiritual life with your neighbor, region, state, country, or in the world.

In Mere Christianity, author C. S. Lewis says, "If you read history you will find that the Christians who did most for the present world were just those who thought most of the next . . . It is since Christians have largely ceased to think of the other world that they have become so ineffective in this. Aim at Heaven, and you will get earth 'thrown in': aim at earth, and you will get neither."

That last line I love so much, "Aim at Heaven and you will get earth 'thrown in': aim at earth and you will get neither." Why not aim big? We need the perspective of Dr. John Edmund Haggai: "Attempt something so great for God; it's doomed to failure unless God be in it." That is a journey worth giving a life to.

## DEFAULT OR DESIGN?

Psalm 90:12 says, "So teach us to number our days that we may get a heart of wisdom."

I want to remember that my days here on earth are numbered. Also, I don't know that number. There will be a final day. Your book will have a final page. Our lifestyle can bait us to focus only on the next five minutes. But what if we lived as though there were a set amount of days left? We know this is true, but we tend to defer thinking about it until later.

Architectural plans take into account all of the specifications before digging the foundation. The pace of the race is determined by its length. Authors and speakers have outlines that specify where they want to go. Begin on the final page.

What if there were only three, maybe four, things you could say with your life? Would you want those things to be said on accident, or would you want to pick the ones to be said?

With life, the messages that last aren't always the last thing said. A legacy is what a life says the loudest. We can now—in this moment—begin to design, shape, and revamp our legacy.

In one of his most famous sermons, known as the Sermon on the Mount, Jesus offers a very poignant teaching. Matthew 6:24 says, "No one can serve two masters, for either he will hate the one and love the other, or he will be devoted to the one and despise the other. You cannot serve God and money." He didn't say you can't serve God and the Devil. The old King James version of the Bible says it this way: "You can't serve God and mammon." Mammon essentially means money, possessions, and stuff. Jesus argues that our stuff is the chief competitor to Him. Let me paraphrase, "The chief competitor to living a life that matters is money, possessions, and stuff."

That verse scares me. And it should scare those of us who are affluent, right? If affluence is more than enough, then I have plenty of things to pull me away from what matters most. I have reasons with zeros behind them to pull me off track. Yet

E. Stanley Jones, who has been called the "Father of Modern Mission," said in light of that verse, "You cannot serve God and mammon, but you can serve God with mammon." I love that line.

Rudyard Kipling wrote a beautiful poem that helps me set the standard for the kind of person I'd like to be and the way I manage my time. I encourage you to read it aloud, slowly, and to repeat it more than once. Find a place where you can be alone and give it your best orator's voice as you think about how you set and follow your priorities.

### IF - by Rudyard Kipling

If you can keep your head when all about you
  Are losing theirs and blaming it on you,
If you can trust yourself when all men doubt you,
  But make allowance for their doubting too;
If you can wait and not be tired by waiting,
  Or being lied about, don't deal in lies,
Or being hated, don't give way to hating,
  And yet don't look too good, nor talk too wise:

If you can dream—and not make dreams your master;
  If you can think—and not make thoughts your aim;
If you can meet with Triumph and Disaster
  And treat those two impostors just the same;
If you can bear to hear the truth you've spoken
  Twisted by knaves to make a trap for fools,
Or watch the things you gave your life to, broken,
  And stoop and build 'em up with worn-out tools:
If you can make one heap of all your winnings
  And risk it on one turn of pitch-and-toss,
And lose, and start again at your beginnings
  And never breathe a word about your loss;
If you can force your heart and nerve and sinew

> To serve your turn long after they are gone,
> And so hold on when there is nothing in you
> Except the Will which says to them: 'Hold on!'
>
> If you can talk with crowds and keep your virtue,
> Or walk with Kings—nor lose the common touch,
> If neither foes nor loving friends can hurt you,
> If all men count with you, but none too much;
> If you can fill the unforgiving minute
> With sixty seconds' worth of distance run,
> Yours is the Earth and everything that's in it,
> And—which is more—you'll be a Man, my son!

Hear that last segment of the Rudyard Kipling poem again:

> "If you can fill the unforgiving minute
> With sixty seconds' worth of distance run,
> Yours is the Earth and everything that's in it,
>
> And—which is more—you'll be a Man, my son!"

May that be true of us! May we be the ones who fill the unforgiving minute; may we press into what truly matters.

## EVALUATION

Let me end this chapter by encouraging you to evaluate. This book is not a monologue, but an invitation to dialogue. Write the parts of the book that only you can write—through notes in the margins, conversations over coffee, or keeping a journal. The thing I love about a good book is that it forces you to think. Here are a few good questions to think about:

1. How have you viewed success in the past? How have you experienced the letdown with the view upon arrival?

2. What about this book so far do you agree with? What would you change?

3. When Bible verses were quoted above, what was your response? Do you view the Bible as a different kind of book—why or why not?
4. Think about legacy. What inspires you? What gets you excited? What do you fear happening?
5. What are the areas of legacy where you want to have a more compelling vision?

In the next chapter, we'll talk through how we sell ourselves on ideas, we'll examine how the limited audience in financial discussions affects us, and we'll consider how our decision-making paradigm is altered by having more than enough.

## Suggested Reading

*Your Life… Well Spent* by Russ Crosson

*How to Be Rich* by Andy Stanley

*Finishing Strong* by Steve Farrar

*The War of Art* by Steven Pressfield

*Purpose-Driven Life* by Rick Warren

*Halftime* by Bob Buford

*From Success to Significance* by Lloyd Reeb

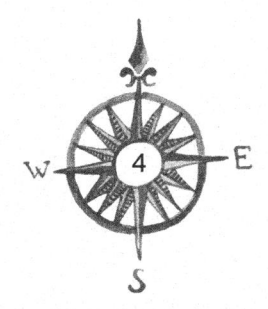

# OH, THE LIES WE TELL OURSELVES

*"You are only as sick as your secrets."*
- Alcoholics Anonymous -

*"I love money. I love everything about it. I bought some pretty good stuff. Got me a $300 pair of socks. Got a fur sink. An electric dog polisher. A gasoline powered turtleneck sweater. And, of course, I bought some dumb stuff, too."*
- Steve Martin -

*"Riches and abundance come hypocritically clad in sheep's clothing, pretending to be security against anxieties, and they become then the object of anxiety. They secure a man against anxieties just about as well as the wolf that is put to tending the sheep."*
- Søren Kierkegaard -

One of the oddest things about money and affluence is how rarely we truly talk about it with others. Chances are, nobody really knows how much money you make or what your net worth is, unless your profession requires that it be disclosed. If you are in sales or you are part of an egalitarian physician group, maybe someone else knows your ballpark salary. But for most of us, most of the time, we are the only ones who know how much we make or what we own.

Most likely, your parents don't know your income, and your pastor doesn't know your net worth. Your best friend or a sibling might have a vague idea. And, if you work with financial professionals to help manage your taxes and investments, they will center on one of three things when talking about money: how to make it, protect it, or increase it. Rarely will financial professionals discuss the other side of being affluent. They may not even know about the other aspects of affluence, especially if they are on the outside looking in. Some aspects of being affluent only become clear after you experience them.

---

MAYBE SOME OF YOU HAVE A PROFESSIONAL TEAM WHO JUST WANTS YOU TO HAVE MORE MONEY SO THEY GET PAID BETTER. THEY MAY EVEN ENCOURAGE YOU TO BUY THE NICE CAR SO THEY CAN RIDE IN IT OR BUY A BIGGER HOUSE SO THEY CAN VISIT YOU AND MEET THERE (OR GET PAID FOR SELLING IT OR FINANCING IT).

FINANCIAL PROFESSIONALS MAY LIVE VICARIOUSLY THROUGH YOUR WEALTH. IF THEY ARE NOT "ONE OF YOU," THEY ARE PEERING FROM THE OUTSIDE IN. BECAUSE THEY ARE NOT AFFLUENT THEMSELVES, THEY CAN HAVE A WARPED VIEW ABOUT THE FULL ASPECTS OF MONEY AND MAY NOT BE ABLE TO ADVISE YOU IN THE MORE HIDDEN AREAS OF IMPACT.

---

## WHAT HAPPENS WHEN WE ARE SILENT

Many affluent people are in the dark about money conversations; they simply don't have them very often, and when they do, it is often only to address one small aspect of their assets or financial planning.

The effect of being in the dark—of being silent about money matters—is that mold can creep in and grow. Untested thoughts that would appear nonsensical if dragged into the light of day seem to make sense in the dark. This is a breeding ground for the lies we tell ourselves.

Those lies begin with the idea that money isn't an appropriate topic of conversation—ever. As psychologist Dennis Pearne has pointed out, "Money is one of our last taboos." Although we may not realize it, we are likely passing this attitude down to our children as well, simply by not saying anything. Pearne notes, "Children assume that if there's something you don't talk about, it must be bad. Their unsophisticated logic moves quickly from, 'I have something that's bad' to 'I must be bad.'"[17] This progression from "I shouldn't talk about money" to "I shouldn't have money" to "I'm a bad person because I have money" is not unique to children. Many adults harbor the same thoughts and feelings, sometimes without being fully aware of it.

For example, I recently sat down with a very intelligent specialty physician. He impressed me. I think most people would be impressed by him. He has good looks, a great career, and a sharp wit; he has always been at the top of his class or peer group. When he left medical school, he had his choice of specializations, which is certainly not the norm. He is seen by his friends as the financially savvy one and is sought out often for advice. Even though he's been successful, he isn't arrogant. He is down-to-earth and approachable. He's a guy anyone would love to spend time with.

But in spite of all he has going for him, I found he had quite a few disconnects regarding financial things. He knew the academic information—he could quote the experts, even Nobel Laureates in economics. But when it came to living out the knowledge, he hadn't taken the step of applying the information to himself. Or, rather, he thought the conventional wisdom didn't really apply to him. In short, he was telling himself lies.

These lies were connected to how his situation connected to the conventional wisdom. He said to himself, "My situation is different. These rules don't apply to me. I am a special case." He could tell me all the reasons this was so. He was acting like he was nine feet tall and bulletproof.

In reality, he had bought the wrong investments at the wrong time and for the wrong reasons. He was ready to spar in defense of his position—the boxing gloves were off, and he could fend off true wisdom with erratic punches of slight mistruths. But in the end, his position just wasn't defensible. He didn't know as much as he, and his friends, thought he knew. Or rather he knew too much: he thought these rules didn't apply to him.

I'm certainly not picking on him, because I've done the same thing. Correction—I do the same thing. They say doctors are the most difficult patients. Counselors are the worst counselees.

Financial professionals, then, must be the worst with their money. This is just a reminder that knowledge about financial information isn't the only thing that's needed. If information alone were the cure, then psychologists would have the best marriages, pastors' kids wouldn't rebel, and investment advisors would all be able to retire early. Instead, we also need the skill of applying that knowledge to our own situation—without allowing subtle lies to creep in.

## ONE-SIDED ARGUMENTS

Have you ever had a one-sided argument with yourself? These happen to me all the time. A one-sided argument is an exercise in self-deception. I tell myself everything I want to hear, and I conveniently forget everything I don't want to hear.

I like to say that we are all experts at selling to ourselves. For me, I like to sell myself extra dessert. Or another tap on the snooze button. Or postponing that workout until next time.

I can even support my decisions with research. I'm pretty sure I read a study online that compared processed foods to other kinds of foods and determined that what mattered was calorie count, not kind of food. I'm also pretty sure I read a study online (although I couldn't tell you its larger point) about the benefits of eating with other people. So I tell myself it doesn't matter so much what I eat—that extra dessert is just a choice I'm making so I can spend more time with these good friends!

I quote these kinds of studies all the time. But I'm not even sure what their details are or whether they come from a reputable source. What I am sure about is that they provide a convenient way for me to mask the lies I'm telling myself. They give apparent legitimacy to a choice I wanted to make whether or not those studies were relevant or even true.

Can you think of some areas where you've sold yourself a half-truth? Why did you upgrade the countertops, select your last car, or shop at some fill-in-the-blank expensive store? What about the way you spend your time, money, or energy? Can you think of any situations where you have told yourself (or your spouse or your colleague or your client) one thing, while you really knew that something else was the driver of your decision-making?

Pastor and author Tim Keller says, "In the short run, self-deception is wonderful. In the short run, just closing your eyes is great—but in the long run it kills you."

I justify a new car purchase based on these little lies. It is about our current car failing us, or the gas mileage I seek, or the one feature that's now in the newer model, right? Or is it because I want to feel important when I drive up at the light and have others look at me?

With a private plane, it's said you don't justify it based on the math; you rationalize it with time and feelings. Or with home purchases, we emphasize how much we will be entertaining so that we justify the need to get a bigger house. I spiritualized buying a house. I used the excuse that we host church meetings to defend my preference for more square footage. I pretended that I needed a bigger house for Jesus, when in reality I wanted a bigger house simply to have a bigger house. Is that how it is with you?

I do not mean I'm against all non-essential purchases. But

I do mean we may not be fully honest about why we choose what we do. Our motives are usually more complex than we acknowledge.

With our decisions, it is easy to surround ourselves with our own thoughts or with advisors who tell us only what we want to hear. It is very easy for me to say my house decision is based on lowering my taxes or buying a bigger house to entertain in or, in my case, having a bigger house for Jesus.

But here's the reality. A bigger house might have some benefits, but it would also almost always bring higher taxes and other expenses. I don't know if you can relate to this, but I don't think I'm alone in rationalizing these decisions. I often repeat the same things again and again until they sound like a mantra. Then I believe the lie.

I recently talked with a client about his home purchase, and he said about five times in the meeting that he and his family were buying a bigger house now, actually more than they could afford, "because I don't want to move twice." Every time he was tempted to buy a smaller house, he would repeat, "I don't want to move twice." There were more options this couple had outside of moving twice, but he was stuck on that line. When we repeat these lines again and again, it is amazing how quickly these things start sounding logical.

These repeated lines of self-deception can even start to feel like a press release.

## THE PRESS RELEASE MINDSET

In today's media-soaked culture, the press release is a staple. And the lies we tell ourselves are like our own personal press release: they consist of only the best things we want to say about ourselves. All the negative perspectives have been edited out.

Picture the last incident with a congressperson who did something stupid. Or an athlete caught using illegal substances. What did they say? What did they do? If they are like most people, they sat down with an attorney or group of them and said, "How are we going to spin this?" Then they put out a press release, an edited version only showing the good stuff.

A well-known cardiologist I know was sued for wrongful death and taken to trial. The attorney representing the family of the man who died did his best to position the deceased to be a family man—sharing how much his children depended on him and how much family responsibility he had. The attorney wanted to show how much his life was worth. In response, the cardiologist did the same thing. He took his kids out of school and had his wife walk in with the four of them in tow at every break, even making a scene while handing over the kids back to the wife. A few times, the youngest even cried, not wanting to leave Daddy. They were both positioning their story like a press release to the jury.

This kind of positioning isn't always bad. But it's also not always showing others who we truly are. We show what we want. Dave Gibbons describes this phenomenon in his book *Xealots* this way:

> Far too often, though, we try to bury our weaknesses. We see them as abnormalities that people shouldn't see. We cover up the parts of our lives that seem weird, freakish, or offbeat. The parts that make us beautifully unique, we hide. Instead, we showcase our strengths. We

strive to prove that we are just as good as everyone else. We highlight the things that make us acceptable in the eyes of the world. We inflate the things that normal people applaud. We become good at creating facades. We develop a habit of projecting an inflated image. What a waste of time.

Don't we do that? Don't we position our story to others and even to ourselves? We show them what we think they want to see. I do this all the time. With new friends, I tell certain stories. I don't lead with taking ballet in college, but instead with my FBI story or some recent exploit. We tell ourselves little lies to sell ourselves on how we really want to act or buy or behave. Last night I worked hard and late—so I deserve to snooze now.

One of my favorite press release lines is, "I buy quality." Because who doesn't like to buy quality? Do you think the poor people at the Bargain Store are saying, "quality, nah . . . I like cheap crap." Or my grandpa's line was, "I buy once, so I buy well." And there is truth to those lines. But when we overuse or use them to hide our real motives, then we are selling ourselves a load of lies. I've personally found I say those things to give myself permission to buy more expensive things, even when doing so might be out of line with my long-term plan or family goals.

## SO DO I NOT BUY "QUALITY" STUFF?

I'm not saying to never buy a big house. I did. (And why right now do I want to preface "big" as being a relative term? Is it so you'll see me as more noble somehow)? I'm not saying to buy things of lesser quality just to prove a point. What I am saying is to make sure you are aware of the real reason you do things. Below is a good exercise to help assess this, and I encourage you to be honest with yourself. If you make financial decisions on behalf of or in partnership with anyone else, you may want to include them in this conversation, too.

Discovering the real reasons we make decisions we have can be a powerful exercise. So ask yourself and answer honestly:

- What is the real reason I stay later at work? I may say it's for the kids, but how much money do they really need to be happy?
- What is the real reason I got divorced? I needed to be happy, right? But what are the other reasons?
- What is the real reason I bought that expensive bottle of wine on the double date? The maker of the wine list is developed to make you choose a certain way; the second cheapest bottle on the list in each category is almost always the one with the highest profit margin for the restaurant. Nobody wants to buy the cheapest wine, right? But you bought a bottle to show something. Was it because you could afford it? Or because you are the kind of person who knows wine?
- What is the real reason I don't call my daughter back? Relationships aren't simple, but I'd be willing to guess there are reasons you don't want to say out loud.
- What is the real reason I upgraded the kitchen countertops? I know, resale value of the house, right? But outside of the logic given by the salesperson, what else went into the decision?
- What is the real reason I bought my current house? The school district is good, wanting to be hospitable, wanting to be the house your kid's friends play in. But did you say the non-noble reasons out loud? Did you say any of the crass ones?
- What is the real reason I buy so many shoes? Shoes are great,

but is there an identity and self-worth issue here? Do I wear a certain new pair around that crowd, or specifically wear that pair around her?

- What is the real reason I drink at night? Yes, I need a nightcap to sleep, and who doesn't, right? But could it be other issues?
- What is the real reason I bought my current car? I know, gas mileage. The environment is huge for all new car buyers for a season. But did I address the ego play, or the identity issue? Or did I justify it with needing to look a certain way for work? Or what people expect of me since I've now arrived.

Could there be an insecurity you are trying to mask? What role did loneliness play in this? How did "he" or "she" impact this decision? What other people were factored into these choices? Could it be you are still trying to please your father or your mother? Is there a sin rearing its ugly head?

There almost always is a grain of truth in these lines to make them more believable. Flat-out lies are easier to reject. But deceit is . . . well, more deceptive. Which of these lines about justifying decisions do you use? Take some time be honest.

I rarely find that our decisions about money and finances are purely one thing or another. I agree with Ron Blue when he says, "There is no independent financial decision." We can think we are being pure or rational, but many times if left to ourselves to make the decisions, we simplify the other point of view. We say, "Obviously this is true for most people, but for me, it's different. For everyone else getting out of debt is good; it is different for me."

It doesn't sound noble to buy a big house because I want people to notice me or people to think I'm well-off. It doesn't sound virtuous to buy an expensive car to feel important. It doesn't sound rational to get a surgical procedure because you feel old compared to your son's mother-in-law. It doesn't sound spiritual or honorable to make decisions based merely on what I want. I can easily make myself think I'm making decisions based on others, Jesus, or gallant aims, when, in reality, there is another side factoring into my decisions.

> **REALITY CHECK: IF YOU HAVE NOT ADMITTED TO MAKING A BUYING DECISION BECAUSE YOU SAW SOMEBODY ELSE WHO HAD IT, I THINK YOU AREN'T COMPLETELY HONEST WITH YOURSELF. IF YOU HAVEN'T SAID THAT YOU MADE A FINANCIAL DECISION BASED ON A SALES PITCH OR A CAR DECISION BASED ON A COMMERCIAL, YOU'RE NOT BEING FULLY HONEST. IF COMMERCIALS DON'T CONVINCE US, THEN WHY DO ADVERTISERS SPEND SO MUCH MONEY ON THEM? YOU'VE HEARD ABOUT THE MILLIONS ADVERTISERS SPEND FOR A MERE 30 SECONDS DURING THE SUPER BOWL, RIGHT? IF YOU HAVEN'T GIVEN ANY REASON FOR BUYING CLOTHES OR SHOES, OR PURSES, OR WATCHES, OR A BELT–OTHER THAN I DESERVE IT OR I LIKE QUALITY– THEN YOU ARE NOT BEING COMPLETELY HONEST. TAKE A MOMENT TO REFLECT MORE DEEPLY ABOUT WHAT DRIVES YOUR SPENDING CHOICES.**

Where is the truth of our decision-making? It's somewhere in the middle. Did I use my house for church events? Yes, at one point we held three weekly events there. Did and do we entertain? Yes, we often have family reunions, and family and neighborhood kids frequently run around in our halls. But the understated motives also played into it. I'm sure, at some point, I wanted to be in the nice neighborhood to be noticed, to look well-off, to be in a good school district, to be among "nice" neighbors, and so on. When my wife and I made the decision, though, I don't know if we even brought up those thoughts.

What's my point? We need to move into a place of honesty with ourselves about how we make decisions about money. If we are going to make lasting change, we need to stop repeating silly arguments and look at our motives and what is at stake. We need to sort through the difference between the truth and the lies we tell ourselves.

## ONE DAY, SOME DAY

We talked last chapter about success being a direction. Yet it's not easy to see some paths that we are going down. It's easy to see the paths others are following. It's really easy to see the path my kids are going down. But I give myself a pass because one day in the future I'm going to change. "I'm not going to live forever in the party scene. I'll settle down one day." Or, "My lifestyle isn't bad because I'm starting out in the career." We say, "This is just a season of craziness." Or, "When I get settled in, then I'll change my spending habits." But if you continued on your current trajectory, where would you more likely end up?

Think about a physician in medical school. Talk to one about how tough med school is. It's tough. They all think it will get better in the future. Dr. A. P. Derdeyn, author of an article called "The Physician's Work and Marriage" in the International Journal of Psychiatry in Medicine, described physicians as having a "point of arrival" mentality. Once they enter residency, they think, then things will get better. Then, when they are in residency, they are sure, things will lighten up. If possible, though, residency only gets worse. Then, physicians continue to tell themselves that when they enter practice . . . or when they get established in their career . . . or this new job will allow me to . . .

Don't we all do that?

What happens when we are going down a path and we don't like where it's taking us? What happens when our kids don't want to hang out with us anymore because we worked too much and were noticeably absent during their pre-teen and adolescent years? What happens when your marriage gets rocky and you don't really like the other person, but you think you still love the other person? What happens when you get to a point where it seems to not be working out? There is always hope.

We need to change.

It has been said, "The only one who likes changes is a baby, and even then they cry." So how do we make effective changes in our thinking? How do we challenge our simplistic defenses? How do we avoid lying to ourselves?

It is so easy for faulty thinking to creep into our pattern of making decisions. Money decisions are even worse, since, for the most part, we rarely talk to other people about money. What happens when we have thoughts about money that get left unchecked? We often repeat the same lines again and again. Left unchecked, we may find we believe the lies.

## A TIP-OF-THE-NOSE PROBLEM

Being honest about how money affects us is often a tip-of-the-nose problem. You can sort of see your nose without a mirror, but not the full tip. It is simply too close to your eyes. We can see other people's nose tips, but not our own. If you concentrate, you can see the edges of your nose, but our brain edits them out. The tip of the nose just blends into the picture, and pretty soon we can't even see our nose edges in our normal vision. We need another person, or a mirror, to help us see certain problems.

You may call these "plank-in-the-eye" issues. Jesus once encouraged his listeners to take the plank out of their own eye before trying to remove the speck from someone else's. We can see someone else's speck, but not our own plank. How we can we be so blind to our own faults!

What tip-of-the-nose problems are you aware of in yourself? Or what tip-of-the-nose problems do you think other people would identify in you?

Our tip-of-the-nose issues with money are often secret thoughts that we are unaware of. Our thoughts aren't often reflected on, but assumed. How much thinking have we really done about our thinking?

I recently found this poem by Ella Wilcox Wheeler. It draws out the idea of secret thoughts so well. Listen carefully or even read this out loud.

### "Secret thoughts" By Ella Wilcox Wheeler

I hold it true that thoughts are things.
Endowed with bodies, breath and wings,
In that we send them forth to fill
The world with good results—or ill.

That which we call our secret thought
Speeds to the earth's remotest spot,
And leaves its blessings or its woes
Like tracks behind it as it goes.

It's God's law. Remember it
In your still chamber as you sit
With thoughts you would not dare have known
And yet made comrades when alone.

These thoughts have life; and they will fly
And leave their impress by-and-by,
Like some marsh breeze, whose poisoned breath
Breathes into homes its fevered breath.

And after you have quite forgot
Or all outgrown some vanished thought,
Back to your mind to make its home,
A raven or dove, it will come.

Then let your secret thoughts be fair;
They have a vital part and share
In shaping worlds and molding fate—
God's system is so intricate.

## EVALUATION

1. In what areas of your decision-making paradigm do you receive the least outside input? How does that impact your ability to

more forward and make changes?

2. In what areas are you most likely to continue to tell the outside world the "press release" version of your past? Are you being fully honest with yourself in the areas that matter?

3. Go back through the questions in the chapter and those statements around justifying our decisions. Spend some time reflecting on the hard questions. Identifying ulterior motives doesn't necessarily mean those motives are wrong. But a first step toward purposeful decision-making is identifying all of our assumptions about money, possessions, and things, and putting each of these to the test.

4. What was your takeaway from the "Secret Thoughts" poem? Is there one "secret thought" that has influenced your decisions that you can now identify as a partial lie?

In chapter five, we'll dive into how to attack the root of these problems, how to contend with the soul with honesty in these areas, and how to guard our hearts against the pull towards the insignificant.

## Suggested Listening
*Your Move* with Andy Stanley
*Living on the Edge* with Chip Ingram
*Timothy Keller Podcast* with Timothy Keller

# ATTACKING THE ROOT

*"There are a thousand hacking at the branches of evil to one who is striking at the root."*
- Henry David Thoreau -

*"Honesty is the first chapter in the book of wisdom."*
- Thomas Jefferson -

*"What is necessary for a person to change is awareness of himself."*
- Abraham Maslow -

I have a friend who doesn't weed his lawn too often. A quick glance at their bushes will show you my—I mean his—lack of discipline in weeding. Okay, it's me. I hate weeding and, really, yard work in all its forms. So I looked out my window last week to see six-foot tall thistles in my yard. Seriously, six feet. I looked them in the eye . . . without bending over. Do you know thistles actually have a pretty flower on them if you let them grow long enough? When I tried to get rid of them, I learned thistles not only have with pretty flowers and nasty thorns, but the root system is hardy. Once it has established its root, removal is no simple task.

Just like we attack rampant weeds, we need to attack the root of the issue surrounding money and having more than enough. I'm sure I will oversimplify this discussion for some. But what is at the root of our decisions? Is it emotions that drive us? Is it our logic? What are the things that influence our soul level on how we think and act?

These root and soul-level influences are spiritual, heart-level, and foundational. Our family of origin and past play large roles. This is not simply modifying behavior or cutting off the branches. We can't simply cut off the thistle's flower; we need to address the issue deeper down.

## HOW WE RESPOND TO PAIN

Our reactions and emotions are in deep places most of us don't fully understand, particularly the profound emotion of fear. In the introduction of the book *Amusing Ourselves to Death*, Neil Postman brings out this unique insight comparing Aldous Huxley's and George Orwell's classic works. He compares their fear. Let's listen in.

> What Orwell feared were those who would ban books. What Huxley feared was that there would be no reason to ban a book, for there would be no one who wanted to read one. Orwell feared those who would deprive us of information. Huxley feared those who would give us so much that we would be reduced to passivity and egoism. Orwell feared that the truth would be concealed from us. Huxley feared the truth would be drowned in a sea of irrelevance. Orwell feared we would become a captive culture. Huxley feared we would become a

trivial culture, preoccupied with some equivalent of the feelies, the orgy porgy, and the centrifugal bumblepuppy. As Huxley remarked in *Brave New World Revisited*, the civil libertarians and rationalists who are ever on the alert to oppose tyranny "failed to take into account man's almost infinite appetite for distractions." In *1984*, Orwell added, people are controlled by inflicting pain. In *Brave New World*, they are controlled by inflicting pleasure. In short, Orwell feared that what we hate will ruin us. Huxley feared that what we love will ruin us.[18]

It's not my goal to settle that literary debate. I tend to think there is genius in both Huxley's and Orwell's observations. Our reactions to pain and pleasure both play essential roles. In my experience, there are at least three soul-level influences at the root of our actions: 1) how we respond to pain, 2) how we relate to pleasure, and 3) our past patterns.

Fear plays into all three in a unique way. Fear, in essence, points out danger and risk. Fear keeps us away from physical cliffs but also emotional and spiritual ones. Fear makes us hesitate to share sensitive information around people who will hurt or abuse that information. Healthy fear points out our limits and imparts wisdom about dangers. Psalm 111:10 says, "The fear of the Lord is the beginning of wisdom."

Our fear often sheds light on our true identity.

## HOW WE RELATE TO PLEASURE

It's amazing how saying yes to a pleasure can shape us. Food, wine, chocolate, sex, fine dining, coffee, vacations, pain pills, and many other good things can turn on us. Freedom and control are tricky surrounding our pleasure. When I say yes over and over to anything, it can turn into habit. Try cutting coffee, and the headaches and fatigue come roaring like a lion.

When good things like comfort or food become ultimate, their power is huge. Our pleasure-seeking, freedom-loving "yes" has now turned into an addiction. We started drinking because we could get away with it, and now we can't sleep without one. We sought sexual freedom, but now our urges control us. Pleasure can easily become an idol.

## OUR PAST PATTERNS

Our past patterns are also key. Over time, our reactions form deep patterns. Our past is often the best indicator of the future.

Jay Stringer says it this way, "We look to the past not to find excuses for reprehensible behavior, but because narrative holds the key to unlocking destructive patterns and implementing all future change." These patterns then help us see some of the logic. The legendary seminar professor Howard Hendricks is famous for saying, "Experience doesn't make you better. Only evaluated experience makes you better." Taking time to evaluate our experience is wonderfully beneficial. Careful evaluation allows wisdom to shed its needed light on our emotions and experiences.

Learning the correct lesson from the past, however, is not simple. "We should be careful to get out of an experience only the wisdom that is in it—and stop there," as Mark Twain once said, "lest we be like the cat that sits down on the hot stove lid. She will never sit down on a hot stove lid again—and that is well; but she will also never sit down on a cold one anymore." Learning what the actual lesson is and not extraneous points requires, as Professor Hendricks says, proper evaluation.

## NEW PERSPECTIVE

When you encounter new ways of thinking, it is easy to throw them out based on your existing pattern of thinking.

Much of our thinking on money—in particular in relation to our kids and giving them an inheritance—is driven by ideas that aren't founded on rational thought. Why do I give all my kids all my money in three installments? How much is enough for each heir? Should it be always equal? If I challenge that notion without giving you reasons to change or a larger purpose, I'm merely stirring the pot or meddling. But if we talk through legacy and why we give kids an inheritance, then after much discussion and wisdom circle back to actually setting up our estate, we might indeed find that boilerplate method of thinking to be too simple.

Is the solution to just follow your heart? That's one of Hollywood's favorite solutions: be true to you.

The problem with this proposal is that, as we talked about last chapter, we are good at lying to ourselves. Listen to some of the strong biblical warnings about trusting your heart. Proverbs 4:23 says, "Above all else guard your heart; for everything flows from it" (NIV). That is a steep warning. And how can I guard my heart without knowing it? Guarding is a very different posture than following.

Also, hear this warning from Jeremiah 17:9, which says, "The human heart is the most deceitful of all things, and desperately wicked. Who really knows how bad it is?" (NIV) Deceit is hard to see as well. Flat-out dishonesty is much easier to see than deceit. This warning is saying that my heart is deceiving, and its audience is typically me. Think back to our raccoon with its hand in the trap holding the shiny object we talked about the prologue. How do we know we are not currently snared? Do all people who are snared know they are? If my heart is prone to deceiving me, how would I know?

Proverbs 14:12 also addresses this, "There is a way that seems right to a man, but its end is the way to death." And again in Proverbs 12:15, "The way of a fool is right in his own eyes, but a wise man listens to advice."

The heart and emotions have a place. Their place is not the engine but rather the caboose. Rational thought and principled purpose make much better companions for your major decisions. For you science folks, let your prefrontal cortex take over and not your amygdala. If we by reasoned thought, truth, and love speak into our heart, emotions will come into line.

## IDENTITY

We often take our identity from our strengths or what makes us look good. I'm never going to see myself as a golfer, because I'm terrible. I find my identity through my strengths. Don't you?

What about those of us with more than enough money? On the higher end of the wealth spectrum is the Forbes 400 list, and there are people and families who try very hard to get on or off the list. Why? Identity from money is huge.

Our identity in our affluence usually isn't directly related to cash in the bank, net worth statements, or accounts. We may keep score by comparing net worth, but we usually know someone else with more, so that's not the game we play. If our number is lower, we are quick to find another way we are better. Our identity may be how we handle money, how we spend it or don't spend it. It may be how much we earn, how good we are at investing, or how hard we work to protect our money.

Our identity and our personal worth can be tricky when money amplifies our heart. And it's easy to move our identity off what we want it to be and onto what those around us think it should be. Peer pressure didn't end at high school, right?

Let me tell a story about how affluence shapes identity. I recently lost my wedding ring. It was the first time in 13 years that this had happened. Looking to replace it, I went shopping. It was in the "pinkies up" part of town. The shop was very high end, and I was feeling what I call "the pull." My identity was being challenged, and I was thinking how I could live this kind of life. But I always have taken pride in being the kind of guy who does not wear Gucci, Armani, etc. I constantly take personal pride in "not needing that kind of thing to make me feel important . . ." Remember, I'm Americanized Dutch, so part of my identity is being frugal.

But the store's styling was very well done. The lighting was just right, the music soft and elegant. The salesman was called Brenton with an accentuated "T"—come on! Even his name was good for his job. I was standing there, and I felt a pull.

I'm all about advertising and marketing. Those industries are helpful. But it starts with one premise: you lack.

You, the customer, need what we, the company, have here.

My friends at Harvard Business School might argue that there's more to marketing than that, and they would be right. But showing what we lack seems to be the starting point of many sales pitches.

Those of us who live in advertising-saturated environments are bombarded every day with messages shouting to us about what we are missing. The newer, the shinier, the upgraded, the faster, the name-branded, the organic, the more comfortable, the long-lasting, the market-researched, the academically proven, the doctor-recommended—the better.

Yet, here I am with my old, smelly, outdated, obsolete, worn-out, used, unpolished, out-of-fashion, last-year's-color, dull, and off-brand stuff. I see the new, and I feel the pull. The pull makes me feel as though I'm less for having less. The pull reminds me I'm not up to date. The pull draws me into a bigger, flashier version of myself. And I buy and upgrade, or I dream about buying and upgrading.

The pull is heart level. The pull is strong. The pull works.

Tim Keller said, "Every person, religious or not, is worshiping something to get their worth." This identity issue is spiritual and root level. This means that it requires soul-level solutions.

## How do we find root-level solutions to resist the pull?

### 1. Challenge your Assumptions

There are some assumptions we make that need to be

challenged. How much money should I spend on a house? How many vacations should I take a year? How do I relax? What kind of car should I drive? Some of our thinking about money has never had a push back from an outside source.

Regarding vacation and relaxing, for instance, I'm all for it. But does our current system and style of living allow us to actually rest? Or do we, like most people, need a vacation after coming back from a vacation? There is little margin in our current pace of life.

The concept of margin is intriguing. I first heard this idea applied to life in a book titled *Margin* by Richard Swenson. Walk with me through this concept that challenged my assumptions on rest and work.

Notice for a second this page. Would it be easier to read if the words went all the way to the edges? The words stretched all the way to edges would be unnerving. But isn't that how some of us live? We live straight to the edge. Few of us have margin in our schedules, finances, relationships, or life in general.

Swenson defines margin is the distance between power and load. Power is our total resources, energy, and ability. Load is the demands on our resources, energy, and ability. Margin is simply power minus load. The more margin or power left over after our load, the better we will find life to be. The book is worth the read.

In regards to rest and vacations—maybe you need to take more of them. Or maybe you've been American-Dream-retired for years and you are bored. Then maybe you need to challenge yourself and get involved.

My point? Challenging your assumptions can have a really

good result.

## 2. Be Honest with Ourselves

I've found I use several techniques to hold truth at bay. The two I use most often I call "the Stiff Arm" and "the Straw Man." Let me explain.

### The Stiff Arm

The Stiff Arm is a move in football where the ball carrier sticks his arm out to try to keep the tackler away. I use the Stiff Arm whenever I'm in a situation where I feel challenged. I'll say "that won't work for me," or "my situation is unique," or "I know someone else who needs to hear this." I do this all the time with good sermons that strike to too close to home. I say, "oh, I wish he could hear this" or "I hope she is listening." Those lines keep me from dealing with the conviction of the passage.

In saying those lines, I am trying to keep tough questions or discussions at arm's length. Where in reality my situation is not that unique; I may be unique, but my situation is not that unique. Ask any counselor how many truly unique situations they have heard. It's not that many.

### The Straw Man

Similar to the Stiff Arm is the Straw Man. A straw man is a simple argumentation tool; you've probably seen it in a sales setting too. It's a weak or exaggerated position set out to make an alternative position look more attractive. I do this one all the time. When challenged to spend more time with the family, we'll say, "I'm busy," or "I'm important," or "I'm not a stay-at-home dad" or "the bills don't pay themselves," or "well, I'm not perfect but…"

None of those are arguments. It's funny, because some of those lines might even be true. But Straw Men fail to address the tension over spending more time at home. They make me feel better in the moment but don't address the underlying issues.

Budgeting is a struggle for my wife and me (and by struggle, I mean we constantly find ways to not do it). I don't know how many times I've said, "I'm not an accountant" when confronted with the idea about keeping better handle of my money. My line about not being an accountant is the straw man position used to downplay my need to keep better track of my money.

These might not be your defenses; find yours. I'm sure you do something to avoid dealing with the hard truth. Figure out what lies you tell and learn to apply truth.

**3. Seek Outside Help**

Some issues need outside input. These are the tip-of-the-nose problems. We have to include someone else in the discussion. A spouse, a coach, a counselor, a friend, a professional—any and all of these people might be appropriate.

I would wager if you choose well, the friend you open up to will already know some of what is going on. And chances are, he or she can even relate to parts of you are going through. In his letter to the Corinthians, the Apostle Paul says, "No temptation has overtaken you that is not common to man. God is faithful, and he will not let you be tempted beyond your ability, but with the temptation he will also provide the way of escape, that you may be able to endure it" (1 Corinthians 10:13).

Unpack that with me. No temptation is unique. If you think the word temptation here is weird, then "struggle" or maybe "the lie you've been telling yourself." People have shared with me things they've shared with no one else. And guess what, it looks an awful lot like the struggles I've faced and the ones we've mentioned here. Sure, there are unique bits, but the heart of each temptation is more similar than dissimilar.

God is faithful. It's worth saying again. God is faithful. He is there. He can be trusted. And "…he will provide a way of escape…" There is hope. There is a way out. There is a solution. There is something refreshingly human about connecting with someone else on these issues. There can be a wonderful bond found when you trust and share on this level.

## 4. Guard Your Heart

There's a proverb in the Bible that says, "Above all else guard your heart; for everything flows from it" (Proverbs 4:23, NIV). The pull happens at the heart level. My identity flows from my heart. My words flow from my heart. Why do I not take steps to guard it?

Safeguards on the heart are great to have, and I'm going to suggest some practical safeguards. These issues might not be your issues. But I hope the specifics of another may inspire you to action.

- In order to avoid greed, several families have placed a spending cap on their lifestyle. Andy Stanley says, "Greed is the assumption that it is all for my consumption." One family who made roughly $2 million a year placed a limit on spending for themselves at $150,000/year. They then, with great joy, give away the extra to causes they love.

- Another family liked the idea of a spending limit, but approached it differently. They decided to give away net worth above a certain limit. In their case, they decided to give away anything above $5 million in net worth. While still mid-career, they gave away a percentage of ownership of their business to a donor-advised fund. (A donor-advised fund acts as a mini-family foundation without as much of the overhead and legal requirements).

- Another good friend was sick of advertisements telling him when to upgrade his car, phone, and lifestyle. He made a commitment not to upgrade anything needlessly. This was tested when the back of his cell phone fell on the cement. The back of the glass broke and "spidered" out. He now calls it now his "Spider-man-edition phone." He bought a cover for the back and kept it for one full year, giving the money he would have spent on the phone to a local charity.

- Another family adopted the no-upgrades policy and only replaced broken things. They found fixing them to be rewarding. They heard this idea while in the middle of planning for a huge remodeling project. They decided much of their motives were to look good for others. When they wrestled through this in their heart, they gave away 50% of the project to build homes in Haiti and continued on with a smaller amount of home renovations. They then took a trip to Haiti one year later to visit the homes they built. The father still recalls that as one of the best things he did for his family. When his kids get together, they all agree their favorite family trip was that one, not the countless trips to beaches and mountains. That one trip, he says, really solidified their family identity and love for each other.

- I know a man who struggles with being fully honest with financial decisions. He runs all decisions above $3,000 past a trusted friend. The man wanted to buy a new car. The friend asked why, since his old car still worked. The answer was less than stellar. He ended up waiting on the new purchase seven months. In the seven months of waiting, the money he was saving each month on payments for the upgrade was given away to ministry to great impact. After seven months, he purchased the new car without guilt and also without the assumption that it was all for him. The delay in purchase spoke loudly to his heart and his kids. His son later said this delay in purchasing made him believe his dad really lived out the faith he had been telling him since his youth. He saw how much his dad wanted the car and how his dad was living what he taught.

- The one antidote for greed I know is giving generously. I know many who give systematically a percent of income, net worth, or assets. They figure Jesus was right when he said where your money goes your heart follows. They think of giving as a way to move their heart off of themselves and see it as a way to make their world bigger than their house, kids and retirement accounts.

  I have found that giving generously has brought me real and lasting joy. Until you've started to go down the path, you will not understand it. Trust me—giving moves your heart to others better than anything else. Make sure you see what the results are, and I think you will find it to be wonderfully engaging and even addictive.

  I recently asked David Wills, president of National Christian Foundation, what people should do if they don't experience joy in giving. He simply said, "Give more." Then he quickly added, "and give more wisely." Then he outlined the idea about giving wisely covers the "why, how, and where of generosity." Understanding our motivation about why we are giving will help to understand and experience more joy. Giving strategically and systemically and even sacrificially will result in joy. I would add to David's challenge to give in a way where you can see or at least hear the result. Giving can feel like a bill when you don't engage with it and join in with what is going on.

- Get in community. Make sure you have a group of people you can be transparent and talk to about the negative side of money. If you have no one you can discuss the non-noble things about money with, find them.

At first, if you are only honest with yourself, that is a good starting point. But after a while, telling someone else might just be the breakthrough in friendship to push past the varnished and edited life you show now. Vulnerability could move you to a place of genuine friendship and community.

- Find someone with whom you can begin to be financially transparent. This can be on small levels. You could share which ministries you give to with a peer who also is generous. You could find a like-minded financial planner. Give small amounts first. Then give more of your story to faithful people.

- Set an annual giving goal and a lifetime giving goal. This should push you to be creative in your giving. How much time have you spent to give creatively? I know when I want to take a vacation I can find the money. I get creative on where I draw the cash in my budgeting process. When is the last time you were creative in moving money around to give sacrificially?

- One group of business school graduates set up what they call a "Board of Directors for Life." It is what it sounds like. These friends hold calls monthly where they confess new struggles, encourage one another, share parenting wins, and yes, discuss finances. They share an annual financial report with one another, which is fairly detailed, and have committed to living generously. Their close fellowship provides a built-in guardrail against the dangers of money thanks to their close fellowship. With those guardrails, their formal and informal structures help to hold them accountable not to one person's pet interest but each couple's stated goals.

- Finally and maybe most importantly, watch out for rigidly following these safeguards. By following a set of rules, you can be ignoring God's guidance for your daily life. I desire to honor God with everything. In faith as with finances, the principles and safeguards can move me into a place where I follow them as a slight step away from following Jesus himself. Be careful in having safeguards to still seek daily to monitor and guard your heart. Guardrails and safeguards are good, but when you follow them mechanically, it can reduce joy if you aren't watching out.

## 5. STOP COMPARING

In our increasingly globalized society, comparison is easy to do. We see the best storytelling yet listen to dinnertime chatter of our kids. We hear the best sermons online and attend a local church, sitting under, at times, mediocre preaching. Living locally in a global society has a new set of challenges. One piece of those challenges is comparison.

C.S. Lewis puts it this way, "Pride gets no pleasure out of having something, only out of having more of it than the next man. We say people are proud of being rich, or clever, or good-looking, but they are not. They are proud of being richer, or cleverer, or better-looking than others." The thing my heart wants to do is look better than everybody around me. But that is ugly.

One way to guard your heart is to watch out for how you react in comparison. When you compare to someone worse, you walk away placated. When you compare to someone better, you feel less than them. Either way, when comparing, there is little win. I know who not to compare my work ethic to, who not to compare car knowledge with, or my workout habits to, etc. We typically only compare to others that make us look better. What is up with that?

It can be easy to sit in inaction based on comparison, instead of pushing yourself based on who you want to become. Lazy habits can be justified simply because I know someone worse. I walk away feeling as if I'm better but further into isolation and deeper into a judgmental heart.

If I'm striving to be the best daddy I can be, that motivates much better than crudely checking that I did more than my father or thinking I'm better than the little I know about my neighbor. That again is the Straw Man showing up. Are you supposed to be some weird version of your parents, or are you called to be there for your family? Are you supposed to be average or the best you can be? It may be trite, but if you placate yourself with "I'm a better parent than my mother was," you may be right. It just won't help you move the ball down the field.

Think back to the moment you became a parent. Or the last time you saw an infant. I was in the room when all four of my kids were born. I will never forget it. The little arms, fingers, and toes all covered in goo. They were each remarkably beautiful. They were each absolutely priceless to me in that single instant. Nothing could change their value in my book.

Yet what inherent worth is there to an infant? Seriously, what valuable thing do they produce? They eat, sleep, poop, and cry. That is it. Yet there is something within all of us that recognizes the worth, beauty, and value inherent within the humanity of that child. We see value in a baby that is not based on achievement, talent, or action.

Worth is innate within humanity. The Bible tells us that God made us in his image. We are valuable because He is valuable. We have value no matter what mess we've made, or not made, with what is ours. We are priceless and valuable in simply being. Yet we struggle to accept this fact.

We try to earn worth or prove worth. We think that we can't be very worthy, since such great worth is common: "Great,

I'm valuable, just like everyone else on the planet." We want to be anything but common. We want to stand out. We are okay having value, but we want more of it than the next person.

When we try to add value to our being, it is a play to control our situation. We try to add more worth to ourselves. To use another term, we try to add to our self-esteem. Chip Dodd says it this way, "Self-esteem is something we manufacture in order to create a sense of control or power. It offers a false sense of worth based not on our inborn gifts, but on our achievement only: 'I did; therefore I am.'" This should not be. Instead, we can say, "I am; therefore I will now do." Our action, then, is not done to prove anything. Our action stems from our already proven worth.

## EVALUATION

1. Identity is tricky. Where do you find your sense of worth or identity? Is it money? Accounts? Net worth statements? Your parenting skill? Your job?

2. Do you find that comparing leads to making you better or worse? More specifically, with each important area, does feeling better or worse depend on whom you compare yourself to? How do you decide which standard or example to follow? How do you know if you are falling short or exceeding?

3. What do you do to avoid pain?

4. What do you do to guard your heart? Are there safeguards you need to put in place? Did any on the short list strike a nerve or inspire you to add a similar safeguard?

In chapter six, we'll walk through the negative sides to affluence, and you might find yourself saying, "I'm not the only one." We'll also look at a few of the reasons why wealth pressures us, isolates us, makes us arrogant, and, in general, pulls the heart to places we don't want to go.

## SUGGESTED READING

*The Voice of the Heart* by Chip Dodd
*Boundaries* by Drs. John Townsend and Henry Cloud
*Gospel in Life* by Dr. Tim Keller

# THE FLIP SIDE OF AFFLUENCE

*"[In a shipwreck] one of the passengers fastened a belt about him with two hundred pounds of gold in it, with which he was afterwards found at the bottom. Now, as he was sinking—had he the gold? Or had the gold him?"*
- John Ruskin -

*"Probably no man ever ventured to mourn at not having three eyes. But anyone is inconsolable at having none."*
- Blaise Pascal -

*"For every one hundred people who can handle adversity, there is only one who can handle prosperity."*
- Thomas Carlyle -

Many affluent feel poor since they don't have loads of cash immediately at hand. In other words, their lifestyle has crept up with their income, and they feel cash poor even while spending and enjoying a lot of stuff, vacations, and a nice house (or two). My friend and author Tom Martin calls this a "preferred form of poverty." It is completely a self-made problem due to extravagant lifestyle. But it is a problem.

Experience has shown me that no one feels rich, even those with liquid cash in excess. Consider Russ who, combined with his wife, earn more than $750,000 a year, but feels he's middle class because he shops at Wal-Mart and, at this time in his life, does not own a yacht. Pretty much all observers outside his head would say he is no longer middle class. Having the proper perspective is important. Since we live in context, we need to address these issues in context. My kids don't know our house as big or small. It's simply a home. Perspective on that for them is hard to see. The same is true of our relative wealth.

There is an internet phenomenon called "first-world problems." The concept is funny and points out the funny parts of being affluent—things like "my ice cream fell to the ground before I could eat it all" or "my diamond earrings keep scratching my smartphone." How about "my neighborhood is so new my old GPS can't find it?" Or "the dialogue in the movie is too low, and the soundtrack and sound effects are too loud." Those are funny, but the real problems with affluence aren't typically quite as laughable.

We've already spent a lot of time on the flip side of affluence, but I want to continue down that path a bit farther before offering more solutions. Truly understanding the depths of the problem and dynamics surrounding wealth is an important step in coming to grips with this area of your identity.

## BUT I DON'T STRUGGLE WITH THAT!

Philosophers, preachers, teachers, observers, and bloggers love to talk about materialism and greed. Materialism is a focus on stuff, on money, and on what it can bring. But in my day-to-day world, I don't spend too much time thinking about materialism. Here in America, we are arguably the most affluent society in the history of the world. In the book *Origins of Wealth*, Eric Beinhocker argues that "over 97 percent of humanity wealth was created in the last 0.01 percent of our history [in other words the last 250 years]." But I don't often live daily in light of that fact. I just turn on my indoor plumbing and complain that it doesn't get hot fast enough to wash my face or take my shower.

I spread drinkable water on my lawn without a second thought. My cars live in better "housing" than most of the world. I can swipe a piece of plastic and have people make me a meal, cut my hair, or clean my house. I have access to endless information with the click of a mouse, yet I get irritated when the webpage takes longer than two seconds to load. I get fresh produce from around the world consistently and complain the strawberries in January don't taste like they are fresh off the vine. Can you relate?

Daily I ignore this unique affluence and expect, even demand, the best. I overlook the beauty of a sunset, a child's laugh, and a friend's time. Why? Because I'm busy, focused on other things. I don't stop to be grateful. I'm caught under the influence of affluence. Having more than enough cash for basic living has moved my heart away from gratitude. It has changed me.

Those who grew up poor or in a middle-class background and now find themselves in the deep waters of affluence often express an odd difficulty with the other side. James Grubman calls these people "immigrants to wealth." In his book *Strangers in Paradise*, he states that about 80 percent of the wealthy are the first generation to be so. He compares the transition to affluence like that of an immigrant. It's a wonderful analogy. I would argue that many make this transition without any guidance. The immigration process takes them by surprise.

There is a great thought in Dietrich Bonhoeffer's *Life Together* that applies here. Bonhoeffer was a pastor in Germany at the time of Adolf Hitler. He was a leader in the Confessing Church, which opposed Hitler's changes. This thought on the "Wish Dream" applies to any church, community, or relationship, and it is, I think, one of the most profound and helpful things he wrote on community. Here is a snippet:

> Innumerable times a whole Christian community has broken down because it had sprung from a wish dream. The serious Christian, set down for the first time in a Christian community, is likely to bring with him a very definite idea of what Christian life together should be and to try to realize it. […]
>
> […] Every human wish dream that is injected into the Christian community is a hindrance to genuine community and must be banished if genuine community is to survive. He who loves his dream of a community more than the Christian community itself becomes a destroyer of the latter, even though his personal intentions may be ever so honest and earnest and sacrificial.

Listen to this part again, "Every human wish dream that is injected into the Christian community is a hindrance to genuine community." I love that. The ideal version of what community should be gets in the way of what the actual community we face looks like. Expectations are huge, right? A "wish dream" of marriage can get in the way of our actual marriage. This applies to marriage, parenting, finances in general, and especially to having more than enough money.

The ideal of what affluence should have provided me doesn't look like what it does provide me. This shows up when I hear an immigrant to wealth say, "I never thought it would turn out like this." I've heard countless clients say, "I thought I'd be able to do more monthly in my budget with $20,000. I thought I'd feel different. I thought it would bring me closer to my peers who are making the same amount." Well, where are those ideals coming from? And more importantly, are they accurate?

Let's look more deeply at money, its effects on us, and how it can skew our perspective. Along the way, be sure to think about how these apply for you in particular and not just the wealthy in general.

## 1. Affluent People Feel the Pressure to Have it All Together (a.k.a. the Camelot Syndrome)

One of the problems with affluence is that the affluent feel pressure to appear like they've got it all together.

I call this pressure "the Camelot Syndrome." The roundtable and the castle look great from the outside. On the inside, fighting abounds, and Lancelot is sleeping with the king's wife! There are issues, even if they aren't showing.

This is remarkably common. The perceived pressure from wealthy people, institutions, and traditions is great. And yes, the pressure felt from the non-affluent people can be high as well. The affluent feel the need to hold a "stiff upper lip."

This tendency to show only the parts that make us look good

isn't new. Facebook, Instagram, and social media didn't invent this issue. But they certainly gave us a new way to struggle with it. This propensity to hide from each other is a result of what happened back in the Garden of Eden. Ever since then we have been trying to show only certain parts that make us look good and hide others that aren't as acceptable.

Affluence uniquely presses on this struggle. Oftentimes relationships suffer as we get higher up the social economic scale. In part to pacify our guilt and justify why we made those decisions, we show that everything is going smoothly. After all, if I thought early on that money would make my problems go away, I'm now at the point now where the problems should be gone. But they are not.

**2. Affluent People are Lonely**

Simply put, the top of the hill has fewer people. But don't expect the less affluent to have any empathy for your loneliness. And trying to impress is not a great way to cultivate true friends. One man shared this very struggle, since he can't exactly open up about his struggle with giving his kids too much inheritance with a friend from church who is losing his job. They are very different struggles. He struggles, for the most part, alone.

I think the Camelot Syndrome above and the issues below show why the affluent are lonely. The additional reality is, affluent people don't know who to trust.

Wealth and success tend to isolate, and lots of wealth and success will eventually insulate.

One man I interviewed shared that a decade can go by in a

heartbeat, and you look around and there is no one who is your close friend. This is all too common.

Recall Wayne Jr.'s comment we shared in chapter 2, "I was happy, but I was never fully satisfied." That, from my experience, is quite common. If you ask affluent people, they say they are "happy." Yet there is often this low-grade loneliness that can fester without fully being aware of the loneliness.

As you get older, friends decline in general. Add an increase in wealth, and it happens sooner. Psychologist James Grubman argues that once income rises above $75,000 happiness declines. What about friends?

A financial planning friend tells the story of a very wealthy man. They were in the planning process when all of sudden the man left the conversation. They paused a moment and asked him what he was thinking. After a lengthy pause the man shared to his wife, "Remember when we lived above the old ice cream shop? Do you remember how many friends we had calling to hang out? I don't know if I can honestly say that now I have even one close friend." This is unfortunately not uncommon for affluent people to say.

### 3. Affluent People are Funny about Money

We understand the impact of things like compound interest and the effects of inflation. I have a friend who grew up thinking she was poor since her mom would hesitate to buy things like bananas or milk when they got to a certain price point. She went home from the store thinking, "We must really be poor since we can't afford bananas."

I have a client who has shared, "It is easy to walk into a room and think, wow! I'm the wealthiest person here." Undoubtedly, it's a shallow way to both look at yourself and others. But the truth is, money can be a dividing factor, from both sides.

**4. Affluent People Struggle with Judgment**

To get and keep your assets, you have to say "no" sometimes. Saying "no" to something makes you judge someone who says "yes" to the same thing. I know a man who liked to take very nice vacations. His close friend liked to go hunting; a successful trip meant bringing home a "trophy." See how they might tend to judge each other? We need discipline in order to gain wealth. Andy Andrews says, "Self-discipline is the ability to make yourself do something you don't necessarily want to do, to get a result you would really like to have." As we grow our wealth, we need to make ourselves say no to certain purchases, expenses, and opportunities. We can then begin to feel proud of saying "no" to opportunities and expenses others around us see as a need. We can be proud of not being at the Country Club, not being a big golfer, not owning a timeshare, not having a second home, not wintering in Florida, or not eating out often.

Another man I talked to was proud of still personally mowing his own lawn. He actually has lectured several friends about teaching his kids a lesson about hard work through lawn care. To him, having a lawn guy was almost a sin. There are other ways to teach kids about hard work, but he judged his friends for using a lawn care company.

Wealthy people have a tendency, then, to take pride in one area in particular. They may go on lavish trips and eat fancy food, but take pride in not wasting money on alcohol. One man I interviewed shared with pride that his home only cost him $15,000 each year to maintain since it was paid off. Can you see him judging the man who has mortgages on three homes with lots of toys?

Chip Dodd says, "Judgment is a form of trying to stay safe and not be taken advantage of." Our fear of the unknown and fear of losing that are held somewhat at bay when we judge. It's a temporary win, but a long-term loss. Discernment, however, is another story. As Dodd says, "Discernment is seeking to see clearly the attitudes and behaviors of another for the purpose of [...] seeking truth, not safety." To Dodd, it's about not attaching worth to those noticed differences. Discernment is used to gather info, but judgment separates.

### 5. Affluent People Feel Guilty About Being Affluent

Being wealthy in an age where the whole world is a click away means stories about poverty and pictures of poverty are common and come right into our homes. Having wealth and comfort and doing nothing about poverty and suffering can create a good amount of guilt. Guilty people tend to stop hanging out, to start insulating themselves.

### 6. Affluent People Can Struggle with Being Arrogant

While it's easy to point to someone else as arrogant rich person, it can be helpful to turn the mirror to ourselves. Wealth often accompanies leadership and success. As I've said before, people start behaving differently around wealthy people, giving them more attention and deferring to them. We can start to feel like, since we have earned this money, we deserve to be listened to, obeyed, and praised.

This behavior only divides us more from other people. We want to be seen by others as a person, not a wealthy person. We don't want money to fully define us.

Being treated poorly for our wealth can reveal our arrogance. Today, some believe it's evil to be successful. We know it's not. Politically, it is not popular to be rich right now. The "one percent" movement is very divisive. It is creating some really high walls.

Pride and arrogance are hard to see in ourselves. We often need to consult someone else we trust to help us identify arrogance so that we can fight back against it.

## 7. Affluent People Tend to Fall into Hyper Budgeting or Hyper Spending

We often switch back and forth between extremes of spending and saving. For example, I have clients who will pay big bucks for a particular car but then insist on not paying for a haircut personally.

I've never met a person who thinks they spend a lot. We all justify our purchases before and especially after we buy them. We say no to buying countless things, so we feel like we don't spend a lot of money. We also have good reasons for why we own, buy, lease, and use our money as we do.

Behavioral economists will tell us it's common for a person to be okay with spending $4,000 or more to get leather seats in a car, but pause to get a similar upgrade for a leather couch in the house. This is partly because the purchase of a car is seen as a total purchase, not just a single decision. This is why car manufacturers often put their upgrades into packages. You want automatic doors in your minivan? You need to upgrade to the "elite" package that included a bunch of things you might not normally buy.

We put money purchases in different categories. Think about it: my wife and I share all our money, but yet I'm happy when she buys me a present. Why does that mean more to me than simply buying it myself? The money comes out of the same account, right? Mental accounting is different than simple math. My point here is that we carve out money decisions in our head in different ways. We tend to be hyper-sensitive about spending in one area but hyper-willing to spend in another.

## 8. Affluent People Find that Wealth Builds Barriers, Intimidates, and Creates One-Sided Relationships

Wealthism. It's a term not acknowledged by spellcheck, but coined by Barbara Blouin of "The Inheritance Project." Wealthism is the belief that people with money have no problems. The truth is that people with money have largely identical problems to everyone else. Remember, money is an amplifier.

Author and financial planner Jay Link shares a good example of this about a wealthy man and a poor man who both need to fix their garage. What does the poor man do? He calls his friends to come over to help. After all, they will repay the favor someday. He thinks, "If I buy the pizza, we'll call it a day." But he pauses to call the affluent man. Why call a man who doesn't do manual labor to help fix your garage? Why call that friend to help when he gets paid so much per hour?

What happens when the rich man calls his friends? Do they expect to be paid? Do the friends return the favor? They may wonder why they are helping him when he can hire people to do this? It is different.

Affluence intimidates. As an individual's money increases, his or her circle of friends decreases. Building any relationship involves risk; building relationship with someone perceived to be important can feel even riskier, because it is assumed that their time is worth more to them. This creates another barrier to friendships. It is easy to ask a less intimidating person to hang out, watch the game, or go on a double date.

I know when I was interviewing people for the book, there were some I was nervous to talk to. The bigger the person's accounts, influence, and importance, the more intimidating they are. I didn't pause when asking for people I knew and had relationships with already. But the greater the real or perceived importance and affluence of the individual, the more nerve-wracking it is to initiate a relationship.

Affluent people experience one-sided relationships. One of my clients told me about his aunt who is very wealthy, but never seemed to have money with her when they all went out to eat or shop. Is it because she wants to make sure her family is going out to dinner with her and spending time with her simply because they want to be with her? It's important to her to know that.

This happens with friends, too. If your friend is not wealthy, what is the expectation for who pays for lunch? Does the less-wealthy person try hard to grab the check? Work hard not to get the check? Insist on two checks? Sometimes this leads to eventually not going out to lunch at all. Money differences change the dynamic. Wealthy people want to be valued for something other than the ability to pay.

## 9. Affluent People are Very Concerned About Asset Protection

In a nutshell, wealthy people tend to build barriers to the world. The wealthy often feel an intense need to protect their assets, whether it is from fraud, risk of lawsuits, or other risks of loss. Trusting others becomes harder and harder.

Asset protection is basically trying to protect your life from "them" out there trying to get "me." We need to protect our stuff. Part of this is simply prudent. Lock your doors, yes. Follow wisdom about how and when you share, yes. As with home protection and invasion, we need to take precautions to stay safe.

But wisdom needs to be applied to see when our walls keep friends out. Fear-based decisions get you to do dumb things. Fear can masquerade as prudence. Walls intended to be castles can quickly become gilded cages.

Your Asset Protection strategy, though well-intentioned, might not be going over well with your kids. One man shared that their plan for asset protection/estate planning, called a "Family Limited Partnership" or FLP, made his kids feel used. One son said he felt like a pawn in "Dad's game to beat the IRS." There are downsides to certain strategies, the effects of which aren't felt for years. Trusts as a vehicle aren't very trusting. How do you feel when you aren't trusted? Does your current show trust to your children? Or are you building needless walls with them, too?

And who is this vague "them" we feel we need to protect against anyway? Could this line of thinking be a stiff arm to keep possible friends and community at bay?

**10. Affluent People Have Certain Targets on their Back**

A financial planning friend shared this story while at church. He was talking to the wealthiest man in his congregation. A younger man came up nervously to ask him to go to lunch. The response was very quick from the wealthy man: "What are you selling?" The wealthy man clearly thought the only reason this younger man would want to lunch with him was to pitch a project or sell a product. Sound sad?

Over time, people with money tend to believe that everyone has an agenda. With every request it just feels like they're "getting hit up." If an acquaintance calls and wants to ask for advice, is it really going to become a request for money? There is often a track record that suggests this might be the case.

The wealthy have been asked so many times that it is only logical to pull back. It is easy to become skeptical of motives. Yet thinking "they" are trying to get something from you can help create that reality. When I think the worst of others or make it awkward for people to ask from me, it can create more awkwardness. Learning how to say "no" without squashing their motivation to keep doing what they are doing is hard.

I love this thought from Atlanta-area pastor Kevin Myers. "When you chase success before serving people, you can only

Those are new objections to handle.

## 13. Affluent People Find it's Hard for their Employees to be Friends with the Boss

The larger the delta between the salary levels of bosses and their direct reports, the harder it is to build camaraderie. Things just change.

Recently, a former employee called up the office guys for a favor. She needed help moving. As the boss, I wasn't asked to help out. I'm not sure I would have asked either, if I were in her shoes. But I missed out on being able to serve, I missed out on the connection time they had, and more importantly, I saw I was not "one of the guys." I'm in a different category—boss.

## 14. Affluent People Live Almost Exclusively in the Future

I know I'll step on toes with this one. I'm stepping on my own toes, because this is my issue, too. I'm a leader, and I think about the future. I'm always thinking six-months-plus ahead. If you run a division, company, or team you need to think ahead to a certain point. But what happens when you do this with a relationship? What happens when you are so focused on the future that you are not present now? How does this affect your family and friends?

You may be celebrating a win or playing basketball with your son or taking a nice vacation. But there is often a nagging sense of "what do I need to do better next time?" Or do you, like I do, find that every time you are playing ball with your kids that it is somehow preparing them for something else? If I'm preparing my seven-year-old for the NBA, that is a different game of horse than being a silly daddy in the driveway enjoying his son. I find all too often I'm the daddy preparing him for the NBA or college scholarships with tips and coaching.

Now some of you are saying, "Hold up! I thought eternity was supposed to be our focus; now you are telling me that too much future focus is bad?" I hear you. There is a tension here. Not all tensions need to be solved.

To help in dealing with that tension, imagine a ship's captain. Does he get obsessed with the destination and forget to work on today's tasks? No. The destination is quite essential to the daily life on the ship. Knowledge of the destination affects the timing of certain tasks as they reach marks along the way to the destination. But the destination is what drives him to concentrate so hard on the tasks at hand. The length of the journey determines and influences his actions. The destination informs us but doesn't have to control us.

## A STEP BACK

This chapter, like those before, has likely raised some thoughts and emotions in you. Let's revisit the four questions from the prologue in light of what we've already discussed about affluence. See if you can be more specific based on some of the observations listed above.

1. What is working well with how you're currently navigating affluence?

2. What is not working well how you're currently navigating affluence?

3. What about your struggle with affluence is confusing to you?

4. What do you currently need to change in regard to how you're navigating affluence?

## EVALUATION

The most powerful way to go through this exercise is to go through the following questions with someone else—someone with whom you can be fully honest. But taking time to read and carefully go through them with your own thoughts or journal is powerful, too.

1. What have you personally witnessed from the less affluent and their attitudes toward the more affluent? Was it directed to or about you personally? How did you feel? How did you react to it?

2. What resonated most with you about the dark sides of affluence? Which dark side problem made you feel glad you didn't have that problem?

3. What are your feelings about the experiences of the affluent? Did you feel pity? Envy? Jealousy? Do you feel angry with my insensitivity to your problems? Or did it feel like I have been reading your email and texts?

4. Is there a certain relationship that needs mending based on how you've been acting? Do you need to have a conversation with that person about it now?

5. If you could wave a wand and be done with one of these negatives, which one would it be?

Next we'll zoom in on the flip side of affluence for your children, thinking about entitlement as well as other effects of affluence on young souls and minds.

### Suggested Reading
*Life Together* by Dietrich Bonhoeffer
*Golden Ghetto* by Jessie O'Neill
*Navigating the Dark Side of Wealth* by Thayer Cheatham Willis.
*Strangers in Paradise* by James Grubman
*The Price of Privilege* by Madeline Levine
*How to Win over Loneliness* by Dr. John Edmund Haggai

## THE FLIP SIDE OF AFFLUENCE FOR OUR CHILDREN

*"Children are the living message we send to a time we do not see."*
- J. W. Whitehead -
*"A man should never neglect his family for business."*
- Walt Disney -

When I became a daddy, I had no clue what to do. How I found out, too, was a total surprise. My wife's and my theory was to consider starting a family only after we could keep houseplants and pets alive. We were going to first keep the fichus alive, then move on to a puppy, and eventually work up to having little humans in our house. But things changed one day with a little line on a pregnancy test. (To this day, my wife and I are still killing houseplants, although I do take way too much pride in the two plants in my office that are still somewhat green after a year and a half).

I knew what not to say when my wife told me that she was

pregnant. This advice came mainly from a friend who, after being told about his first son, proceeded to let out a few choice expletives. Those words didn't go over so well. His advice to me as a college student was, whenever your wife tells you she is pregnant, act as though it is a good thing, because one day it will be.

The first trip home from the hospital with a new baby feels slightly odd. After all, there's no instruction manual or receipt of purchase. The first weeks, months, and years are an adventure, but also daunting and life-changing. They have a way of challenging you like not much else does.

It seems that there is no shortage of advice both on what you need to do and what you must never do. I needed a filter to sift out the bum advice from actual wisdom. My filter, right or wrong, was to watch other people's kids and interactions. If their kids turned out well and their relationship was fun and seemed like something I'd want, I paid attention.

With that filter up, two pieces of wisdom rose clearly to the top. I call it sage wisdom since it indeed has served me well. One grandpa, with a twinkle in his eye born of undying love for his wife of fifty-plus years, said simply, "The goal is good adults, not happy kids." He continued, "Aim for contributing members of society, not violin maestros, child prodigies, or pro athletes." He set the goal not at the short-term successes like grades, sports successes, or early potty training, but on the long-term matter of good, nurturing adults. That advice has helped me immensely in remembering to focus on the longer-term picture in moments of frustration.

Another piece of advice came from the children's pastor at our church. He and his wife and daughter clearly had so much fun and obviously loved each other. They truly knew how to laugh with each other and at the difficulties of life. He said, "Start early. Seed conversations before they happen." This little piece of wisdom allows for unity on complex issues. If I'm talking with my twelve-year-old about driving, it's a different conversation than when she is turning sixteen tomorrow. Discussing the family view of dating and sex before it comes up is pivotal to avoiding so much heartache, unmet expectations, and shouting.

## THE PATH TOWARD ENTITLEMENT

Parenting is hard enough on its own, but affluence adds its own challenges. What are the other sides of affluence for children? For the most part, we refer to the individual struggles and dark sides of affluence with kids under the banner of entitlement. But it's more than entitlement alone. The effect of affluence on the normal teenage dilemmas and angst can be a powder keg waiting for the match.

Many of us have certain assumptions about the way rich kids will think or behave. Let's review some of these together.

1. **Flat-out arrogance.** Children may justify why they have the best by believing they are better than their peers who have less money.

2. **The need to be treated differently.** Children may demand different treatment because they are a Johnson, or a DeKruyter, or the daughter

of \_\_\_\_. Perhaps other people treat your kids differently in order to get closer to you. Or your kids have observed how others treat you. It's no wonder that they would expect the same.

3. **Weak relational connections.** As parents drive hard to become successful, they often sacrifice their families on the altar of progress and achievement. Oftentimes kids see parents interacting with employees or service staff, but not peers. They need a healthy model of how to relate. Children of the affluent often ask, "Do my friends like me for me or for my stuff? My house? My toys?" Surrounded by a mountain of such cool toys, children of privilege wonder why some acquaintances are so "friendly."

4. **Entitlement.** Children of the affluent may demand the best of everything right now. When they leave college, they feel a right to maintain the same lifestyle and luxury their parents provided all along the way. For most of us, marriage is our first deep experience in seeing decisions made differently. With your kids, they assume that everyone has what they currently enjoy. One wealthy child commented, "I grew up thinking everyone had their family's name on a museum."[19] Why would he think differently, unless he was told?

5. **A lack of respect for authority.** It is common for the parents of the affluent to bail them out. We need to keep up the appearance that all is well in our little kingdom. Affluent children may learn that if they break the law at school or eventually with the police, their parents will bail them out. As a result, they learn to live above the system.

6. **Rebellion.** Arrogance, weak relational connections, and a lack of

respect for authority can lead to rebellion. Many affluent parents have had to sacrifice family time and energy to achieve. As a result, their time away from young children has weakened the relationship. Weak relationships don't show up right away. You don't move immediately from missing one baseball game to a shouting match of "I hate you" by the staircase. The shouting match comes after years of neglect and avoidance.

---

**YOUR CHILD'S SHOUTING AND HYPER-EMOTIONALISM COULD ALSO SIMPLY BE PUBERTY, TOO. DON'T OVERREACT AT THE FIRST SHOUTING BY THE STAIRS, BUT DON'T UNDER-REACT EITHER. THAT BEHAVIOR NEEDS TO BE REBUKED, BUT IT IS IMPORTANT TO SEE THOSE OUTBURSTS AS REVEALING SOMETHING MORE GOING ON. DIG INTO THEIR LITTLE HEARTS AND UNDERSTAND BEFORE YOU SMACK THE RULES DOWN. STILL FOLLOW UP WITH THE APPROPRIATE CONSEQUENCE, BUT MAKE THE EFFORT TO UNDERSTAND THEM AS WELL.**

---

7. **Loneliness.** An event from a five-year-old child's birthday party stands out in my memory, though it has been years ago now. The birthday boy was spoiled. He regularly received $60 toys when out shopping with mom. The boy learned early on he would get the toy of his choice from mom simply to shut him up while out. When a not-so-wealthy friend gave him a relatively cheap gift, he tossed it aside without a thought or comment. The friend's face fell, and a small wall grew up in their relationship. By the time the two friends—best buds when younger—hit the tween years, the wall had become

insurmountable to the point where they have little common ground to build the friendship. That leaves the little rich boy surrounded by stuff, but all alone. Loneliness is an awful pain. Mother Teresa once said, "The hunger for love is much more difficult to remove than the hunger for bread."[20] That is at the heart of this struggle. Money can't replace loving friends and parents.

8. **Materialism.** Stuff is easier to control than people. If your kids have weak relationships, are arrogant, demand to be treated differently, are rebelling against their parents, and are lonely, stuff is what they have left. It is all too common for rich kids to place disproportionate value on possessions above people. Good things, even small things, can easily become ultimate things. Big emotions and reactions that you think are not fitting point to identity issues.

9. **Mental health challenges.** In her book *The Price of Privilege*, Madeline Levine suggests, "America's newly identified at-risk group is preteens and teens from affluent, well-educated families. In spite of their economic and social advantages, they experience among the highest rates of depression, substance abuse, anxiety disorder, somatic complaints, and unhappiness of any group of children in the country." That list is not light or easy to read if you are affluent.

She continues, saying, "[Researchers] find that the most troubled adolescents often come from affluent homes." These children and teens often have access to larger amounts of money, more free time, and less supervision than their peers. They don't just experiment with pot but jump right into the more expensive drug du jour.

10. **A lack of self-control or discipline.** Let's call it lik affluent parents avoid the talk about self-control or we don't have it either. Even if we possess willpow how we arrive at our conclusions. After all, do we need to have our kids see that we took only two vacations when we considered four? Many of the discussions about "reining it in" don't make it down to the kids.

The steps above are the road to entitlement, and, sadly, I have seen far too many kids walk down this road. Parents don't set out to form entitled kids. Let's take a look at how this situation might develop from the mouths of people who have learned the hard way. These case studies are real, but some details have been made more universal.

## Story One: We are Beginning to Struggle Alone More Often

"Straight out of college, we connected with a few couples. We had kids at the same time. That began the discord, but we could have made it through that—yet I make more than they do. I say it's our parenting choices that have pulled us away, but money played a larger role than I'd like to admit.

We've grown distant from our friends. We have not talked openly about many of the money issues. Our friends have seen that as our pulling away from them. Since we are not in community, our kids have drifted out of community, too.

The friends who used to be close now look with envy at our lake house, cars, and private schooling. But we miss the connections. I know money played a role in our not connecting like

Then rebellion happened, this time with a school rule. She was caught skipping class and written up for talking back to her teacher. Then it was shoplifting at the mall. And she even had the cash to pay for it in her purse! We covered it up since we have our image to maintain at the club. After all, it's not my fault she acts that way, right?"

The problems are easy to see in a short story format, but in our own life they are harder to spot. Relationships aren't so black-and-white in person. And we always justify why we do what we do.

The stories we tell ourselves work for a while. But what happens when there is a bump in the road? These bumps can reveal our faulty logic. They show us what is really going on and how close we are to running into our limits.

## HOW DO WE FIGHT ENTITLEMENT?

The first step is to acknowledge that the problems we see in our children may very well stem from our own problems or our failure to take responsibility. It may be that we need to start by asking for forgiveness. We may need a "come to Jesus" apology time. I don't mean the pro athlete or the politician press release apology, "I'm sorry your weak conscience is offended by my actions." I mean a real apology, owning up to my part and asking forgiveness.

I mean

- Forgive me for focusing too much on work.
- Forgive me for ignoring these conversations as you grew up.

- I'm sorry I didn't listen when you said…
- I've been a poor parent when it came to talking about…
- Forgive me for not actually being there for you when…
- I realize I hurt you when…
- Please forgive me. I'm sorry.

Being unable to say "I'm sorry" and "I was wrong" has been the reason for too many lost relationships—personally and professionally.

In addition to looking at your past failures and successes, think about how you can become a more intentional parent going forward. Three focus areas are cultivating contentment, addressing willpower, and following the train of natural consequences.

## 1. Cultivating Contentment

Have you ever read Did I Ever Tell You How Lucky You Are by the well-known philosopher and teacher Theodor Geisel, better known as Dr. Seuss? It's a childhood favorite for a reason. My favorite page reads as follows:

> And suppose that you lived in that forest in France,
> Where the average young person just hasn't a chance
> To escape from the perilous pants-eating-plants!
> But your pants are safe! You're a fortunate guy.
> And you ought to be shouting, "How lucky am I!"

Yes, it's a point argued from absurdity, but it's done well. There are so many things in life that we should be thankful for, yet we've already moved past appreciation to expectation and demand. The appreciate-expect-demand curve is a deadly foe to contentment.

When you first get a new gadget, you love it, right? You appreciate all the time it saves. Then you begin to rely on it and expect it do what it said it would. Then you demand that the stupid thing work.

This is how my first GPS was for me. 1) Appreciate. When the first GPS came out, I loved it. I didn't need to think about where to go anymore. No need to carry a map, a printout of directions. I could just enter the address. 2) Expect. After a while, I began to depend on it. I stopped bringing the back-up maps and printouts. 3) Demand. Can you guess what happened when the GPS failed me for the first time? I was mad, late, lost, and grumpy. I was well past the appreciation stage. I was driving in the middle of nowhere, and it was not helping me!

Kids can get through this curve at light speed. If you don't believe me, try not buying Christmas presents one year, or just a lot fewer than normal. The demand monster will rear up its ugly head fast, hard, and loud. Understanding this curve can better help you shepherd your child's heart back into appreciation. Check that, it also helps me guard my heart back into appreciation and gratitude.

Think about it. Travel is such a luxury of our time. I can hop on a plane and be to a place same day. But I complain about security, the cost and inconvenience of checking bags, the waiting, and the small seat size. Or we complain they don't serve peanuts anymore and lose sight of the fact that we're sitting in a chair —in the air —thousands of feet above ground! Sometimes in order to cultivate contentment, we need perspective and focus.

**2. Willpower**

Raising wealthy children is akin to raising kids in a new land or new country. Old lectures from childhood don't transfer as easily as we might expect. Most non-wealthy families teach self-control as "we can't afford it" lectures. But the wealthy can afford it. These lectures need to move from "we *can't* afford it" to "we *won't* afford it."

In order to argue from a "we won't afford it" perspective, we need to know why. We need to understand who we are as a family.

When we know who we are as a family and have articulated it, the conversations are more predictable. We can move out of a fight or bargaining with our children about the single issue to revisit our family legacy story. The conversation can move to, "Remember our family does . . . our family is . . . our principles are . . . therefore we are not buying/doing/scheduling/upgrading because we are…" All of this is predicated on the idea that we, as parents, have discussed this and worked through our own complicated issues about money.

In his book *The Power of Habit*, Charles Duhigg argues that there are keystone habits. A keystone habit is a consistent habit or routine that impacts many other areas. For example, families who eat meals together at home "raise children with better homework skills, higher grades, greater emotional control, and more confidence." Working out is another keystone habit. People who work out consistently tend to use credit cards less, eat more healthily, show more patience with colleagues, feel less stressed, and are more productive at work.

Research is now saying willpower is also a keystone habit or maybe even the main keystone habit. It's hard to think of an area where willpower is not needed or useful to production and sustained movement. Willpower is vital. How do we get there?

Allowances can help teach about the value of money at age-appropriate level. This is a very basic tool, but it teaches many principles so well. Make sure your children don't connect the allowance to doing a specific task. They work because they are part of the family. You can pay more money for extra chores without increasing the allowance. This key difference helps to avoid parts of entitlement.

When I gave my kids their first allowance, I put out three cups: give, save, and spend. I started by giving five pennies. As long as they put one in save and one in the give cup, I would keep increasing the amounts. I started with five pennies, and my son put three in give, one in save, and one in spend. I asked him why and how he felt about giving it away. He loved it. Then I gave him five nickels, then dimes, quarters, etc. I've found that with all four of my kids, they will continue to give more while I'm giving coins, but when the amount reaches dollar bills, things change. They tend to give less and put more in spend. This is partially due to what you can do with five or ten dollars rather than a few cents. But it was very revealing each time.

Helping kids with an allowance when they are young teaches them how to value money. It encourages saving at an age-appropriate level. "How much is a dollar worth?" and "How much can I afford?" are critical lessons for children of the affluent to learn.

### 3. Natural Consequences

Failure is a great natural consequence. There are some really good ways to teach kids this principle, but letting the consequences of their actions teach them and adding some parental wisdom to the lesson can produce huge results.

For really young kiddos who play in puddles, what better way to allow them to see natural consequences than by letting them remain slightly cold during the rest of the grocery store visit? It is easy for them to connect: you play with water—you get cold later. I don't like cold; next time I'll think twice before I play in puddles.

But teaching this way takes time. When it comes to parenting, one of the biggest problems is the time it takes to set up the boundaries and let kids learn at their pace. One of the scarcest resources wealthy people have is their time. And it is far easier to just do the chores than to follow up with our kids to do them. But what did they learn? How does us doing the chores help them learn hard work?

Here are a few tips on fighting entitlement with natural consequences:

- Match the consequence to the crime. For instance, let your child set their own alarm for school to get ready. If they miss the bus, then bring them late to school. Or if they are late for dinner, serve them cold food.

- Don't let your emotions get involved. Discipline and give consequences immediately. Firm response and quick consequences are best. Time outs, removing privileges, isolation, smack on the bottom, or removing them from the area work well.

- Don't use shame, guilt, or emotional reactions in discipline. When emotions are high, it is easy to manipulate via yelling, shame, guilt, and anger. Loss of a privilege, less time with electronics, decisive action, and so on motivate better than a lecture and yelling.

- Let consequences set the boundaries you want. If you have a child who is leaving their toys all over the place, consider putting all toys left out at night in "family jail." If you set up the expectation clearly that all personal items and toys left out will have to be bought back with their spending money from the parents, what a great way to motivate kids in the right direction! Once charged money for toys, they learn quickly. If money is less of a felt pain point, then find the thing that works. Take away time on their phone or with friends to find what motivates them best. Action speaks loudly where words can fail.

For me personally, I struggle with raising my voice and yelling too quickly. Shortly after I yelled at my kids recently, someone asked me simply what I had accomplished. I was dumbstruck by the fact that I couldn't answer the question. To me, it seems that when I lose control of my kids, I try to regain it by raising my voice. But as my good friend pointed out, it doesn't really work. It just shows I'm out of control and shuts my kids down. Instead, I need to re-read the list of suggestions above and let my actions teach, not my shouting.

Take some time as a couple to discuss some strategies. Deciding ahead of time with your spouse and getting on the same page is critical.

Once you have standards in place, communicate them to your children. Setting the expectation with the kids is quite important. Knowing what will happen if they break the house rule and following through will teach very effectively. You need to be consistent. Following up on the family rules is critical for success. Having both parents on board saying the same message is indispensable.

---

"FATHERS ARE TO SONS WHAT BLACKSMITHS ARE TO SWORDS. IT IS THE JOB OF A BLACKSMITH NOT ONLY TO MAKE A SWORD BUT ALSO TO MAINTAIN ITS EDGE OF SHARPNESS. IT IS THE JOB OF A FATHER TO KEEP HIS SON SHARP AND SAVE HIM FROM THE DULLNESS OF FOOLISHNESS. HE GIVES HIS SON THAT SHARP EDGE THROUGH DISCIPLINE." -STEVE FARRAR :

---

## THE IMPORTANCE OF FAILURE

Hear how Michael Jordan speaks of failure: "I've missed more than 9,000 shots in my career. I've lost almost 300 games. 26 times, I've been trusted to take the game-winning shot and missed. I've failed over and over and over again in my life. And that is why I succeed."

Watching your children fail is much harder than you might expect. Many of us high achievers solve problems for a living. We need to fight against stepping in, constantly fixing problems, or helicopter parenting. Townsend and Cloud, in their book Boundaries With Kids, have a beautiful exchange that grabs the picture here of letting the child learn through failure. They say parents need to stop "running interference."

Imagine a child late on the project who has to have certain supplies tonight in order to do the project by tomorrow. Instead of running to the store to teach them the lesson that mom and dad will bail them out, what if you responded like this:

"Mom, I need some glue for my project."

"Sorry, dear, I don't have any."

"But I have to have it. The project's due tomorrow."

"What teacher would call and give you an assignment at this hour without enough time to get the supplies?"

"Come on, Mom. She gave it to us at school."

"When?"

"Two weeks ago."

"Oh. So you have had two weeks to get glue and your other supplies?"

"Yes, but I thought we had them."

"Oh, that's sad. Seems like I remember this happening with the felt you needed for your last project. Well, I don't have any and it's past my bedtime. So I hope you can figure out something to make that does not require glue. Good night, honey. I'm pulling for you."

Wow! Now that is teaching the kid to learn how to control himself. It lets him fail early enough in life where it's not too crazy of a consequence, and it's just good parenting.

Struggle is good. Let our kids want, work, and learn. Failure is a great teacher. There is much even in MBA courses and business schools lately about failure being a good teacher. There are loads more quotes from people who have accomplished much about how much failure taught them. What about the child who has cash to help them avoid failure? What will they learn? What lesson is learned when the parent swoops in like a helicopter and bails the young ones (or not so young ones) out of trouble? Money can buy me out of trouble? Is that the lesson you want them to hear?

We teach so much in those moments. Let's teach well.

If you want to do some more serious thinking about how you shape your kids in the areas of contentment, willpower, and natural consequences, I encourage you to take a close look at Appendix B, an exercise that helps you compose your own family legacy story. This can be an important tool for you and your spouse as you negotiate all of the challenges of parenting.

## EVALUATION

Here are some hard things to think about, but I assure you

they are much easier to do now than when you are under the gun in a siege mentality. Thinking about your kids, answer the following the best you can at this stage of the game.

1. Visualize the lifestyle your kids will likely have as adults. Do they each need an equal allocation of your assets? What if you treat each child individually? Would that cause problems? Are the problems worth it?
2. Does your affluence cause your children to be arrogant? Rebellious? Is there anything you can do to change that now?
3. How do you advise your children to think or respond if they ask you questions like, "Does she like me for me or for our money?" Have you ever addressed this feeling with them?
4. Do you give your children more things or more of yourself? Which is easier for you? What steps can you take to forge a better relationship with your kids? Be more in the present?
5. What is your definition of contentment? Has it changed through the years? How are you setting your children up for true contentment?

In the following chapter we'll talk through how to practically implement this advice at each stage in life. We'll consider plenty of field-tested suggestions that are ready to implement.

**Suggested Reading**
*Boundaries with Kids* by John Townsend and Henry Cloud
*Navigating the Dark Side of Wealth* by Thayer Willis

*Children of Paradise* by Lee Hausner
*Strangers in Paradise* by James Grubman
*The Price of Privilege* by Madeline Levine
*Family ID* by Greg Gunn and Craig Groeschel
*The Three Big Questions for a Frantic Family* by Patrick Lencioni

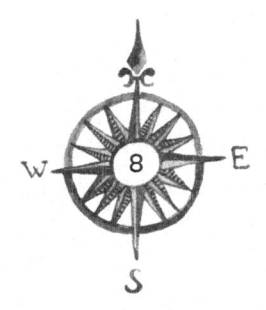

# HELPING OUR KIDS HANDLE MONEY WELL

> *"Good character is more to be praised than outstanding talent. Most talents are, to some extent, a gift. Good character, by contrast, is not given to us. We have to build it piece by piece—by thought, choice, courage, and determination."*
> - John Luther -

> *"If you want children to keep their feet on the ground, put some responsibility on their shoulders."*
> - Pauline Phillips, a.k.a. "Dear Abby" -

Let's admit: there are certain conversations with our kids that are not easy. We often treat money conversations, in particular, like the birds and the bees. I don't know how that went with your parents, but I'd bet for most of us it didn't go too well. It was awkward, done in one big swoop of "get it over with quick," and not discussed again. The result? Let's be honest, both parent and child were happy for those moments to be over. Instead of patterning our money conversations after the birds and bees, we need a new mindset.

## 1. Navigating the Long Journey

Think of a ship. Picture the sails, dead reckoning, navigating by the sun, the rough wooden helm—the whole thing. If we are on a journey across the Atlantic Ocean starting in Lisbon, Spain, the destination matters. Are we going to Miami or New York? They are about 1,200 miles apart. At the start of the journey, however, it's a difference of degrees or a fraction of a degree. Corrections at the start of the journey are a matter of small, measured actions. To arrive at a vastly different destination, you simply make a series of small changes at the correct moments.

What if we approach parenting like navigating an ocean journey? Parenting is a long and often arduous journey. We need to keep in mind the big picture—our seaworthy legacy—in order for the daily grind to make sense. If our goal is to make good adults, not happy kids, then the here and now needs to be viewed in perspective.

## 2. Teachable Moments

Instead of once-and-done conversations, we want to seek out teachable moments for discussing a bit here and a bit there. I'm reminded of the biblical principle of passing on the essentials of the faith: "You shall teach them diligently to your children, and shall talk of them when you sit in your house, and when you walk by the way, and when you lie down, and when you rise. You shall bind them as a sign on your hand, and they shall be as frontlets between your eyes. You shall write them on the doorposts of your house and on your gates" (Deuteronomy

6:7-9). This is seizing teachable moments, not mentioning something once and moving on.

As much as we can see this logically, it is not typically how our parents approached us when talking about money (or sex). As we dive into the issues below, you most likely will need to fight the impulse to lecture once and be done. To actually fix years of accumulated issues, one conversation must be seen as the starting point, not the full solution.

## 3. Train the Mind and the Will

Proverbs 22:6 says, "Train up a child in the way he should go; even when he is old he will not depart from it." Note it doesn't say simply to "teach a child." This type of training is for the mind and the will. They need not only to know the truth, but also to have the wisdom to obey it.

To illustrate, a friend of mine had a child who was honest about being on time-out. The child reportedly said, "I'm standing in the corner on the outside, but on the inside I'm running in the backyard." Your child may be physically present while their will is miles away.

To train your child well requires addressing the mind and the will. Most of us tend to focus on one or the other. Training the will requires soft skills, and the mind requires more logic. Effective training involves doing both well.

---

"YOU KNOW IF YOU'VE BEEN A GOOD PARENT WHEN YOU WATCH YOUR CHILDREN RAISE THEIR KIDS."

**- HOWARD HENDRICKS-**

---

The following bits of advice about how best to do this are gleaned from personal experience as well as many men and women much wiser than me. They are arranged by age level, but only you know how mature your own child is and what is most appropriate at any given stage.

## BIRTH TO 5

**Read books and teach through them.** Reading books on all topics is fabulous, but find a few that talk about financial issues. Or, in the normal course of reading books to your young children, find ways to talk about willpower, self-control, or good and bad choices.

For example, *Corduroy* by Don Freeman is a book I enjoyed even as a boy. I still remember my mother reading it to me and taking me to the department store with a bunch of beds, just like in the book. If I remember correctly, the end of the book has the little girl mentioning she saved up her money to buy the bear. That can be a great springboard conversation to the subject of saving money. Actually that book has several things to teach. One, the mother says no to the daughter in the store. Two, the daughter doesn't throw a fit. Three, the daughter buys the bear with her own money. Four, the daughter cares for the toy by fixing his shoulder strap. And five, it's a cute story on love, on reality, and on dreaming. I'm maybe overselling now, but there are plenty of ways to teach through this one book. Why not talk about one short point each time you read through the book? I know I'm looking for more things to talk about on the books my kids want to re-read again and again. So why not plan it ahead of time?

**An allowance can start at any age.** The best cues on when to start are when your children first ask about money or, if you've passed that point, whenever they ask about a bigger purchase. Smaller amounts for younger kids are just fine. It really is good for them to go into a store with their little sum of money the first time and not be able to buy much of anything.

A key step in the allowance process is that first time in the store when they have money in their pocket. I'd go to the stores you normally go to, not the bargain store. Let them walk down the toy aisle and notice how much things cost. It's healthy for them to notice $20-$50 toys they want with only coins in their pocket. Plan extra time to allow them ask questions, price compare, and digest this new world of money, cost, and not having enough.

**Talk about caring for toys.** A big part of finances is managing and taking care of what you have been entrusted with. It starts with toys. Teach them the verse Luke 16:10, "One who is faithful in a very little is also faithful in much, and one who is dishonest in a very little is also dishonest in much."

**Let each child be their own kid.** Let me tell a story to illustrate this. I once went on a really awesome trip to summer camp. The first time, I had no idea what to expect. I was slightly nervous and timid, but my brothers assured me Camp Barakel was awesome. I had an absolute blast in northern Michigan playing on the lake, learning archery, laughing with my counselor, and doing all the usual camp activities. The next year, however, was different. I think I went in trying to recreate my first year's experience. It turned into a fun time, but it was different. My counselor was not as funny, my archery skills not like I remembered, and the final big camp-wide game I had been looking forward to all year, we didn't even play. My first year's camp expectations were getting in the way of my current camp experience.

I share this in the context of kids because it's easy to stick with the first thing that works. With parenting, I find when I discover something that works with one kid, I at least try to do that same thing for the next. But each child, like each camp year, is different. Let them be unique. Try not to say, "Why aren't you more like your brother or sister?"

My four kids are a blast but are very different. One eats all his Halloween candy within a week, if not a few days. I have another child who takes his time and enjoys a piece a day, maybe even one a week, to, as he put it, "not overload on sugar."

It is easy to go to the fast-candy-eating-child and show him the benefits of the save-my-candy-until-Armageddon-child's wisdom. And that actually is a good lesson for fast-candy-eating children in general to learn. But if you do teach the save-for-later lesson, try to avoid the tool of comparison. Please stop saying, "If only you'd be more like the good save-my-candy-until-Armageddon child." That mentality and wording can damage the strength of the fast-candy-eating child's spontaneous, more artistic, and people-oriented little heart. And even more, comparison language very well may cause a huge rift in their relationship as the years go along.

**Look with a kid's eyes.** Small things at this age are huge to kids. Losing ball games, skinned knees, and popped balloons can be trivial to adults, but they are everything to the child experiencing it for the first time. Remember to see some of life from their eyes. Take those little moments seriously. When you are a big deal, little things are easy to overlook.

I still remember a trusted adult teasing me when I overreacted to a sunburn. I turned out to be allergic to the sunburn cream, so I was badly sunburnt and itchy with pain from the cream. I can see the face of the adult telling me to "grow up and deal with it." Little moments like this affect later relationships.

Men, we often need to hear this one more strongly. I don't get babies. I like to hold them and all, but five minutes and I have my fill. But babies build attachments at these ages. Those attachments carry into the next phase and the next. If you want a great relationship with adult children and grandchildren, love little ones well. If you don't know how, spend time with others who do a good job in this area and see if you can learn some new ways of doing things.

## GRADE SCHOOL, AGES 6 TO 12

**If you haven't already, structure allowance into three groups: give, save and spend.** Begin providing odd jobs so that your children can earn money above their set allowance.

**Teach them to learn to clean up after themselves.** In The Power of Habit, Charles Duhigg argues that making your bed daily is a keystone habit that impacts so many other areas. Some small task to accomplish each day is a great way to start teaching willpower and to give your children small wins daily. Yes, it takes longer now to teach them how to do it than to do it yourself. But in the long run it saves time.

**Make chores fun.** Play good music loudly. Sing and dance with them as you sweep the floor. Teach them to work and like it.

**Let them compare the price of two items** when making a purchase, even with your own money. It's easy to do with gum. Gum is sold in sticks and packs of varying amounts. So, it's a fun game to compare cost per piece of gum with various brands, sizes, tastes, etc. Help them understand how to make a purchase with thought.

**Encourage them to do a lemonade stand or similar venture.** Help them think through costs, supplies, location, and having change ready for the customer. I may be more entrepreneurial than some, but I think this is a rite of passage. My personal rule is, wherever I see a kid with a lemonade stand, I stop and buy.

**Open up a savings account at the bank together.** This can be a very fun time. Think about matching the initial amount they put into the account. (Note: you will most likely need birth certificates and parent signature to open the account.) I would recommend calling your bank before you go and asking if they can do anything special for your child, like explaining briefly the savings book to track the money or, obviously, providing a lollipop (or two).

**Encourage them to decide what they are going to spend before going into store.** This allows them to purchase with a plan and allows them to make better decisions. If you go to the grocery store when you are hungry, do you shop well? A young child in a toy store with money in their pocket is the equivalent of my having fasted for days and then going down the ice cream aisle. Not good.

**Allow your child to spend their savings.** It's important to see the results of saving money on a big purchase. They might choose a bike, a nice dress, roller blades, a big Lego set, or whatever is a larger purchase for them. Saving for college when you are seven is about as fun as a root canal. It is good to see the connection with longer-term savings and the reward for their delayed gratification.

**Incentivize your child to save by offering to double their saved money after one year.** I know double money is not realistic in the real world. But kids at this age (and many grown-up kids) don't understand the power of compound interest. So, pick a rate of return the bank of Mom and Dad gives as interest. See if they will give you the money for another year and let them watch it grow.

**Play games with them.** The Game of Life and Monopoly are great ways to get into conversations naturally with your kids about money. The newer edition of Life says teachers make $100,000 and brain surgeons only $130,000, so it might not be wonderfully accurate. But it still allows you to talk in a less threatening way about money. The games show risk and reward. The Game of Life allows you to talk about kids, career, college, money, debt, and chance—all good things to discuss.

**Clue them into a part of your family's wealth.** They will ask questions about salaries, house prices, and other parts of ine naturally in this stage. Be ready with an answer. If they ask about your income, will your answer be that a teacher makes $35,000 and a lawyer makes $X and not give your salary? I'm not coaching you to either give real amounts or to refrain. I am saying that you will be better prepared if you decide with your spouse ahead of time together, rather than leaving it up to chance in the moment.

When you choose to share actual numbers on net worth or income, it's okay to make them cautious about sharing those numbers with others. Those numbers are private. And that is the key word. When you share about sensitive information with a child you can liken it to private parts on their body. In the same way, we keep private parts on our body covered, certain pieces of information are good to keep private to people or private to certain people who are not in our family. But even with this, many affluent still hesitate to share all the information even with grown kids. I would challenge you that opening up in the correct way can really help to increase honest communication and connection. What reasons do you have to not share these? Is it fear? Insecurity?

**Consider having them develop a spending plan with more than give, save, and spend.** As kids get older, help break out new categories for spending like: Christmas gifts for siblings, birthday gifts for friends, sports gear, beauty and hair supplies, or a book budget, etc. Consider having them give a certain percent to church and then have another segment of money to give spontaneously to the poor or needy.

**Strongly encourage them to serve.** I know this is getting into my values, but hear me out even if this one is not yours. Happiness is not found in stuff or things. Happiness is found in giving yourself for causes greater than you. We all want to matter and have our life echo beyond our last breath. Consistent, faithful service to others moves our hearts to them. Service lessens selfishness, increases awareness of other's needs, and teaches us all that life isn't all about me.

**Encourage them when they do good.** Little hearts are so very open at this age. They are not usually jaded, overly peer focused, or burnt out on life. Encouragement here is huge! Catch your little ones doing good. Try to focus on finding them doing good and not only correcting the bad. I'm horrid here. Within my own life, I focus much more on the negative than the good. I've been reminded (and need to be reminded repeatedly) to see and promote the good, too. Just last night, I taught my little girl how to wipe the table. To encourage this more, I bragged about my little girl to mommy. Guess what she did? She wiped the countertops (poorly) and then swept the floor, too! You get more of what you praise. Celebrate movement! Then, my other daughter got off the couch and cleaned as well, wanting me to praise her to mommy. Encourage good behavior. You will get more of it.

**Praise effort in homework, not results.** If your child got an "A" without much effort in math and worked their tail off to get a "C" in history, what do you do? Praising the "C" feels weird to me. What if you praised their hard work? If they skated through the "A" in math, should you praise them? Instead, ask them questions like, "What did you learn from the 'C'? Did you try hard to get the 'A'"? You can say, "I like your effort in history. Good job on studying for the test. I like how you keep trying."

Self-esteem is not the focus here, but training young ones to try, work, fail, risk, contribute, and produce. A Columbia University study found an inverse relationship with praising intelligence and future results.[21] The study did multiple rounds of tests in fifth graders, with the variable being praising work or effort. When the students were praised for their effort, the test results in the second trial increased by 30%. Those who were praised for being smart decreased by about 20%.

What you encourage and promote will be multiplied. Encourage them to try and put forth effort, and you'll most likely see an increase in effort, which leads to better long-term results.

## TEEN YEARS, 13 TO 18

**Encourage them to get a summer job and fund their Roth IRA.** For newbies, a Roth IRA is a basic investment tool that grows tax free and withdrawals are without taxes if done properly. One main stipulation is the withdrawals start after the age 59.5 with a few exceptions. You need earned income to set it up. You can set accounts up through a professional or simply at any brokerage firm online. Even if you employ the kids in your business, it needs to be "reasonable work." What I mean is you can't pay them to balance your books if they are ten. And you need to have them show up at the office and work for IRS audit reasons. But again, remember we are teaching them to work here and learn about money, not only trying to fund the Roth IRA.

**Talk about a budget for spending.** Consider giving them control of buying their school clothes one semester or a year in advance. Remind them about soccer, basketball, sandals, dress shoes, etc. The key here is, if they blow the budget right out of the gate (there is a good chance of this), don't helicopter in and save them. That only teaches them you will bail them out. Let them learn by wearing beat-up shoes to church or basketball camp.

**Discuss investment accounts and basic investing strategies**, or have them meet with your financial team. Sometimes having you out of the room is helpful.

**Begin to engage them in your philanthropy and giving conversations.** Consider giving them $500 or $1,000 to make their first gift. Have the child outline why they chose a particular organization to give to. Then have the child deliver the check in person. The more they get to the see the results and get involved, the better to encourage them towards lifelong generosity.

**Talk about the family philosophy about debt and credit cards** before they are 18 and can get them. It's amazing how financial education is needed here! Do your kids know credit cards are a form of borrowing? And banks charge interest on loans?

**Go on a family missions trip.** Let them see how other people live. Do hard work together. Cross-cultural experiences can open up their eyes to gratitude and contentment in a way nothing else will. Shared memory and story is also a huge benefit. Think how many beach trips or ski trips you've taken. They tend to blend together after a few years, right? Family missions trips provide memories that are very clear and make for family legends.

**Give them a smaller investment account to manage.** I've heard of one family who gives the children the budget for the vacation and allows them to invest. If their investments do well, then Disney World it is, but if they lose money, camping we will go. This can also be a good way for siblings to talk about priorities and money.

**Talk about your plan for funding college.** My favorite solution is to give them a set amount for college, say $15,000-$30,000/year. If they spend on college above the amount, it's their responsibility. If they spend less, then those dollars are used for a down payment on a house or car when they graduate. But be careful they don't overreact and go to extremes. If you are trying to save money in this way, your child could use this arrangement as an excuse not to go to school. Whatever you decide, communicate the plan before their junior year of high school.

**Remember to encourage and speak life into your kids in all areas of life, financial or not.** Most skills are learned over time, and encouragement is needed along the way. Call them a rock star before they are one.

## 18 TO 25-ISH

**Work together to fund college.** Professors say they can tell when a child has some "skin in the game." Let them pay some of the costs on their own. Lean into the discomfort if there is any. If you disagree on what you are going to do, push past the first pain point. It's okay to follow up with a note later telling them why or reiterating your decision.

The discussion of funding for college will set the tone for future inquiries about money. If you don't fund everything, this might be the first time there is a big disagreement. It will set the tone for future money conversations on a more adult-to-adult level. Be prayerful and careful about this conversation.

**Insist on a summer job in college.** And continue to fund the Roth IRA. Having a boss, limits on their time, responsibilities, and more money is important for building independence. It's also important to have an outside source who will validate your child's work ethic and character.

**Give them a larger amount to manage.** Consider when you will hand over their own accounts, 529, or parts of their UTMAs or UGMAs. Remember here they don't necessarily need to know all the information yet, but they can manage some of their own money with guidance.

**Get more input and involvement from them on your charitable and giving endeavors.**

**Begin thinking about passing the torch for the family business.** One of the most well-rounded wealthy families I know insists their children work their first job not in the family business. This allows the child to gain experience, see the difficulty of the job, and note the difference if they come back into the family business and are now "the boss's kid." It also protects them from the entitled or idealistic gloss common with young people entering the workforce.

**Talk about career decisions.** Speak into money's role in choosing a job. With a career, ordering the conversation around their passion, profit, and competency can be helpful. Finding a career you love, are good at, and can make enough money at can give a sense of calling.

**Begin to let them know what is coming their way from your Estate Plan.** You will do a better job of informing your kids than your attorney will after you are dead. Start young, in small little bits of information, and allow them to ask questions. Take into consideration their point of view, even while taking responsibility for the final decision yourself.

## CAREER, BEYOND 25

**Think about how to communicate with your children about your finances.** At a certain point, your children need to understand the full picture of your family's wealth and estate plan. But know that when you tell your oldest, the younger ones will likely find out some degree of the info you give the oldest. Consider what is private and what should be shared by all.

**Consider establishing family meetings if you have substantive family wealth.** There is much in print on this, so I'll be brief. I've found that giving and philanthropy provide a fabulous common ground for story, dialogue, and fun family memories. Find a common goal, cause, or story to help organize the meetings, which may be more formal or more like a family reunion.

**If you are giving away more than 50% of your income, consider allocating your dollars for your children and**

**grandchildren to give away.** IRS allows for annual gifting each year where you do not have to report gifts under a certain amount. In 2016, the amount was $14,000 per person, or $28,000 if you are married. These amounts ($14k and $28k) can also carry forward five years if you have a larger liquidity event. But these annual gifting amounts are used in many estate plans, so make sure you have coordination with your efforts on giving and estate planning.

**Be purposeful with the stories you share.** Your legacy story can show up here, as we talked at the end of last chapter. The stories we tell show our values. Author Donald Miller says, "A story is based on what people think is important, so when we live a story, we are telling people around us what we think is important." If we tell the story about great-grandpa who came to the United States with only a few dollars in his pocket, that celebrates risk, courage, and daring. If we tell stories that are funny, sad, or embarrassing, it shows our values. The stories we all know but yet never tell show our values as well. Remember and share well.

## EVALUATION

1. Which ideas do you want to implement? Which ideas do you not want to implement?

2. In what ways do you need to tweak an idea to make it work for your situation?

3. Who do you need to talk to about the idea before you implement it?

4. How did your parents talk about or handle money? Is there anything you can learn from your siblings about parenting with wealth? Is money a source of contention within your own family of origin? How do these experiences impact your relationship with your kids?

5. Are you parenting stepchildren or co-parenting with a divorced spouse? How do these situations relate to your decisions about spending, training, and money-related topics? If you are a single parent, how can you be sure that your children encounter other points of view about money and what matters? No matter what your parenting situation, have you actively taken steps to address your children's development in the area of finances?

The next chapter will cover how to handle the built-in friction that comes when principles compete and fight against each other.

### Suggested Reading

*Boundaries with Kids* by John Townsend and Henry Cloud
*The Price of Privilege* by Madeline Levine

### To read to and with your kids:

*Corduroy* by Don Freeman (The book I oversold in this chapter, but it is good)

*Think of Those in Need* by Stan and Jan Berenstain (Many of the Berenstain Bears books provide good teachable moments)

*I Love You the Purplest* by Barbara M. Joosse and Mary Whyte (This cute little kid's book teaches you to love your kids uniquely)

*Oh, the Places You'll Go!* And *Did I Ever Tell You How Lucky You Are?* by Dr. Seuss

*The Toothpaste Millionaire* by Jean Merrill (The best book I know to teach entrepreneurship and business mindset to kids in a fun way)

*One Hen: How One Small Loan Made a Big Difference* by Katie Smith Milway (Great to show "third world" change and leadership without entitlement)

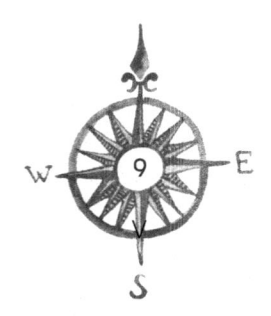

# BEAUTIFUL TENSION

*"I believe that being successful means having a balance of success stories across the many areas of your life. You can't truly be considered successful in your business life if your home life is in shambles."*

- Zig Ziglar -

*"What is necessary to change a person is to change his awareness of himself."*

- Abraham Maslow -

*"Every organization has problems that shouldn't be solved and friction that shouldn't be resolved."*

- Andy Stanley -

Scurvy.

I wager that if you had to guess the next topic of conversation, you would not have picked scurvy. Let me explain.

Scurvy is a disease you can get from a lack of vitamin C. If you don't believe me, Google it. I read about scurvy online, and, as you know, online resources are never wrong, right? Chances are when you think of scurvy, you think of pirates. The problem pirates face is that there aren't many orange trees at sea. With no source of vitamins, scurvy sets in. Like a scurvy-ridden pirate, we have a need for vitamin C. But there is also such a thing as too much vitamin C. You can have an over-abundance of vitamin C just like you can overdose on salt or sunshine. You need some vitamin C, but too much will harm you.

Sometimes we are so out of balance in our personal lives that we sound like a pirate with scurvy quoting medical studies about how harmful excess vitamin C can be. That pirate missed the point entirely.

The real question for our pirates should be how much vitamin C a scurvy-ridden pirate needs. Truly, how much is enough?

How much money is enough? This very well might be the most difficult question I've asked yet.

Built into the question "how much is enough" is a tension. Many of the principles we've talked about create tensions or friction. We want to excel at work and still have a robust personal and family life. Should I give more to my job now so I can build up vacation days and net worth so I can spend more time at home later? Should I get new clients or better service my existing ones?

Some principles appear to be at odds. When we live without the tension, we focus on one side. We can easily get lopsided as a family, organization, or business.

Often, the best solution is not favoring one side or the other, but working to achieve balance. An older word for this is temperance. According to the Merriam-Webster dictionary,

"Temperance is the practice of always controlling your actions, thoughts, or feelings so that you do not eat or drink too much, become too angry."[22] Temperance is just enough, but not to an excess. Temperance is being whimsical but not foolish. It's your head in the clouds with your feet planted firmly on the ground. It's adventurous yet not foolhardy. It's dreaming the someday while living in the now.

## FRICTION CAN BE BEAUTIFUL

Friction isn't always bad. Friction shows up in business via the tension of quality versus quantity or cost cutting versus investing in excellent resources. Oftentimes these aren't once-solved problems that you never have to address again.

Andy Stanley has a perfect question to help us identify and respond to friction. He asks, "Is this a problem to solve or tension to manage?" Many times we see friction as the problem and try to solve it once and for all. That doesn't necessarily work out. We need to live in the tensions and manage them. We need to be content within this beautiful friction.

I don't know the details of your context, net worth, family situation, charitable goals, progress toward retirement, health, or any number of variables. But these two frictions appear in the lives of many and I hope they will resonate with you.

### Friction 1- How Much is Enough?

Like our Vitamin-C-deficient pirates, the question, "How much is enough?" needs more thought. There is a financial point of proper savings. There is a point where clearly you are not saving enough and are presuming on the future. There is also the less-talked-about point of having too much saved. The sliding scale or continuum looks like this:

Hoarding—Excess—Enough —Too little—Presumption

We all have reasons to think we fall into the middle category. But what if we aren't correct? How do we know if what we have is indeed enough—and not too little or too much?

Jesus gives us a very scary parable. It starts with someone trying to put Jesus in the center of a financial issue. His response is beautiful. He gives a warning and then tells a story.

> And he said to them, "Take care, and be on your guard against all covetousness, for one's life does not consist in the abundance of his possessions."

In another translation of this passage the warning is phrased like this, "Watch out! Be on your guard against all kinds of greed." The pastor Tim Keller makes a really good point here. His reasoning goes like this: Why does Jesus say, "Watch out" in regard to greed and coveting? You will never hear Jesus say watch out for adultery. Why? Because you know when you are committing that sin. You will never say, "I didn't know you weren't my wife." But there is something hidden about greed. You need to watch out for it. So we should all start with a working hypothesis that to a certain extent we all struggle with greed.

Let's continue with Jesus' warning. Allow me to tease this out slightly more by giving a modern paraphrase from *God and Money* by John Cortines and Greg Baumer:

> He told them a parable, saying, "The stock options belonging to a manager vested after a major run up share price, and he thought to himself, 'What shall I do, for I already have enough saved to send my kids to college, my house is paid off, and I already max out my 401k every year!" And he said, "I will do this: I will open an investment account and create a passive income portfolio, and I'll exercise my options and put the money there. And I will say to my soul, 'Soul, you have a big enough portfolio to be financially independent; retire early, plan some vacations, and play golf.'"

This is an interesting story. This guy is living the dream, right? In fact, many financial planners today see this as a goal for their clients. You might think Jesus is going to applaud the man. But he doesn't.

Look closely at the wording of the original passage. To the man who built bigger barns, the response is very hard.

> But God said to him, "Fool! This night your soul is required of you, and the things you have prepared, whose will they be?" So is the one who lays up treasure for himself and is not rich toward God.

That is a very scary ending. It speaks very strongly about endless storing up or hoarding. Jesus very pointedly addresses hoarding material goods while not being rich toward God. If this story resembles you a bit, I'd pause right now and think about what you are going to do with what you just read. Does this man's hoarding look too much like your life?

You may say, "I know someone who hoards more than I do, so I'm not that bad, right? They hoard—but me, I'm just careful."

This friction is unique and personal. This friction is not solved simply by formulas, excel spreadsheets, and once-a-year conversations. This one needs to be revisited and pored over. I would suggest regularly praying over and talking about how much really is enough. This is especially true for the very wealthy. If you have more than a million-dollar net worth and have not asked this of yourself, you need to ask it. What amount would be hoarding? Is there an amount of money that would make you feel fully secure?

The friction here is not easy to see. 1) How much is too much? 2) How much is excess? 3) How much is enough? 4) How much is too little? and 5) How much is presumption?

Enough is revealed only when we are living in contentment. Contentment is not in money or amounts; it's about how you feel about that standard of living. Contentment and felt autonomy can be found at virtually any dollar amount. Chip Ingram is right when he said, "Contentment is a learned attitude." The higher the cost of your living, the more pressure you will feel and the more difficult the learning curve will be. You can find contentment in the small things. And you can be really discontented with plenty. Quality of life isn't found in more.

## **IS HOARDING THE RIGHT TERM?**

I know some of you really don't like the word "hoarding." When I speak of hoarding, I mean it in the financial sense. Financial hoarding is when you have excess cash kept for no specific or valid reason. Saving has a goal, hoarding has what-ifs. This hoarding is not to be confused with the hoarding homes on TV shows that are filled with junk and fueled by extreme mental and emotional challenges. In the spirit of Jeff Foxworthy, let me present the less funny (and more challenging) "you might be a financial hoarder if…"

You might be a financial hoarder if:

- You have never been accused by an affluent friend of presuming on the future;
- You have never had to think about what you had to sell in order to give to your favorite causes;
- You have never given sacrificially to the point that it affects another goal or plan;
- You only give mathematically, emotionally, or reactively;
- You have a personal asset that means more to you than you gain by selling it;
- You have a collection you insure;
- You store up shoes, bullets, cars, food, purses, craft supplies, and/or water;
- You never give of your time, emotions, love, or dollars;
- You attach your personal worth to accounts like a scorecard;
- You often use the logic "I might need this later"; and/or
- You have never spent time seriously answering the question, "How much is enough?"

At this point in the book you may be tempted to say, "I know someone who needs to read this." Please try to read this for you first. Try to see if you need to have some personal application before preaching in your head to those other folks. I know it's easier to make this about them. Trust me, I know. In writing this book, my wife and I have had loads of conversations that have impacted me. She'll say, "If you were your client, what would you tell yourself to do?" Not now, dear, I'm busy being a hypocrite!

## LABELS MATTER

A while back, I was introduced to the concept of someone not having an "eating disorder" but "disordered eating." I clearly don't have an eating disorder, that term is very charged. But I think I can say my eating can, at times, be disordered. Labeling is powerful. Changing the label can have a significant impact. So let's not label ourselves as hoarders, but let's admit we have a tendency to hoard. That sounds better while still allowing us to address these issues.

Instead of asking, "Do we struggle with greed or hoarding?" we should ask, "To what extent do we struggle with greed and hoarding?"

If there were a six-point scale with one being totally presuming on the future and six being full-blown hoarder, where are you? No answering 3.5. Admit to a tendency.

Take a moment and think through some key areas and identify a tendency to hoard or presume. When it comes to retirement, do you tend to presume or hoard? With business resources, is there a large and unspecific "what if" category? Do you find it important to keep money for the kids and grandkids with no real purpose? Do you feel challenged by a particular area of consistent spending or saving you don't want me to ask about?

## A SHORT AND CHALLENGING EXERCISE

This isn't an exercise for every decision, but it can be very helpful for bigger decisions or areas where you are prone to self-deception. I know for me that when I find myself repeating lines or making the language sound flowery or salesy, I may be heading toward self-deception. This exercise can lessen the impact of self-deception on decision making.

1. List out the positives of your current line of thinking. Why you are right? What would happen if you were wrong?
2. Then consider the other side. What would a wise person who disagrees with you say are the downsides of your view?
3. List five alternate outcomes. What are other options? Make sure you get out of binary (either/or) thinking. If the decision is bigger, list pros and cons of each view.

I have an acquaintance who is caught in this binary thinking model. Right now, if she can't do her ideal job as a professor, she thinks the only other option is working at a birthday card store. It was her despised job while in high school, and she feels it is below her Ph.D. education. In reality, there are many ways to use her talents, experience, and skills if she can't find an acceptable professorial position.

Also, if the decision is big enough, why not seek outside help? If you are walking through how much is enough for retirement, there are scores of professionals who will help in making sure you are thinking through some needed outcomes, pushbacks, and new perspectives. If you hate fees, many of them will work on a fee-only basis. Ask them to do a simple check-up. You may also want to include a trusted friend or advisor in the conversation.

**Friction 2 – How to Trust without Getting Hoodwinked?**

A few years back I was getting gas for my car. A man approached me with a really good pitch about why he was selling speakers out of his car. He said his work accidentally over-ordered the speakers. His boss was corrupt; he was going to sell them anyway. Therefore, he was selling them now to make a buck, instead of his rich, mean boss. So anything I could give him for the top-notch speakers would be good. Oh, and here is an ATM machine to get cash. I know you are laughing, but I didn't see it coming. Once I saw it for what it was—a scam that I was duped by—it stung. I felt shame. I tried to mentally jump through hoops about how it wasn't a scam to make myself feel better. But the reality is, I was too trusting of my new gas station friend and was hoodwinked.

How do we handle this in daily life? If I err too much on the side of caution and not being duped, will I tend to pull away further, experiencing more loneliness? I want to be in community, but I don't like shame. In other words, we want to be known and loved for who we are without having to hide anything, and yet not be burned in the process of opening up. Sound impossible? We'll unpack some more solutions for building community in the next chapter. For now, let's focus on the tension part of this.

This binary tension can be felt powerfully with the affluent. The children of the affluent also are often left wondering if they have friends because of who they are or what they have.

Frequently, the affluent choose to be lonely rather than risk being hoodwinked or taken advantage of. They console themselves, saying "at least I'm not hoodwinked again." Or, "that is the price of being rich." Or "well, it just goes with the territory." But what if you could see friends as liking your stuff but liking you as well? It's not usually one or the other exclusively.

Being taken advantage of feels like a cardinal sin to many affluent people. It means we have failed to steward what we've been given. It also means we aren't as smart as everyone possibly thought we were. Thus, we retreat behind our sophisticated walls and hide. This is really fear showing up in an unhealthy way. We are controlled by the fear of that pain happening again. Anxiety then follows.

We can never control all the outcomes in business or our kids. Our anxiety cranks up another notch. We hide in fear, anxiously avoiding pain and manipulating people around us to have them see only what we want them to see. How exhausting!

With the affluent, our strengths and identity are often most visible in some aspect of wealth. Our worth is not from simply being rich, but from being a good steward, careful with spending, good at earning, and many other things. When we have money, we perceive ourselves as doing well. We may say, "I'm not a good budgeter, but I am good at making money." Or if I didn't earn it, then "I'm good at keeping it, investing it, spending it, protecting it, or giving it." But what fears are behind those strengths? Fears of losing money drive us to protect.

Identity can also be somewhat situational. How I identify my strengths can change based on who I'm around. One of my brothers is far more frugal than I am; consequently, when

I'm around him, I don't think of myself as frugal. Yet when I'm around someone who tends towards spending, I identify as being more frugal.

What happens, then, if my identity is that I'm savvy with money and I get taken as a dupe? We hate being hoodwinked. The core tension point is how we view ourselves. Psychologists call this inner heroic figure our self-ideal. It seems really similar to an identity (or maybe it is the same thing but sounds smarter). Whatever the term, this is where the friction often shows up. This is when we get most frustrated and emotional, when people treat us differently than we see ourselves or differently than we want to be seen. They disagree with my self-ideal, identity, or image of myself.

What happens with my self-ideals and identity when others treat me in a way different than I view myself? Guilt and shame come into play.

Let me tease this out a second. Richard Keyes wrote an interesting article about guilt and shame that has helped me here. Guilt and shame are similar, but not one in the same. Keyes says, "Both shame and guilt are falling short of some standard." Both are wonderfully powerful emotions that are tricky to nail down. Both can also be good for you.

Guilt is tied to a moral standard or an action falling short of a moral standard. I did something wrong. I can feel guilty for lying because I should tell the truth. I can feel guilty for cheating on my taxes because it's illegal. Guilt is attached to actions that break a moral code.

Shame, however, is different. Shame is not necessarily breaking a moral code, although it could happen then. Unlike guilt, shame is more concerned with how we see ourselves. Keyes says, "We feel shame when we (often suddenly) fall short of this model of heroism." Shame comes up when I fall short of my personal heroic standard. Shame says, "I am bad, off, or wrong." People can feel shame about their car, waist size, house, or income. Those aren't necessarily moral issues. There is nothing inherently moral about my car, but one can feel shame because "I shouldn't be driving this clunker" or "I'm driving a nice car while my neighbor has to walk to work."

Shame is attached to the person. Guilt is attached to the action. Shame is about who I am, while guilt is about what I did.

Some guilt and shame are healthy. Without guilt, we would not behave according to any ethical standards. Shame points out where we need to change or are falling short. Shame helps us to recognize our weakness. Pushed too far, shame can lead to rage or sinful pride. Guilt can be pushed to toxic shame. But on the face they are good indicators of problems.

## FOR THE MEN

For the men who don't want to do emotions, vulnerability, and "shame stuff" with your loved ones, your kids, or your wife, let me push you. Think for a second. They will open up to someone else at this soul level. Are you okay with that person not being you? Are you okay with your wife opening her soul to the handsome, rugged, strong, fill-in-the-blank dude, who is not you? Get over talking about what makes you uncomfortable. Share. Be touchy feely. Get deep and speak about the profound and intimate.

## FOR THE WOMEN

For the women who don't want to do emotions, vulnerability, and "shame stuff" with your loved ones, your kids, or your husband, let me push you. Think for a second. They will most likely open up to someone else at this soul level. Are you okay with that person not being you? Are you okay with your husband opening his soul to the gorgeous, slender, attractive, fill-in-the-blank chick, who is not you? Get over talking about what makes you uncomfortable. Share. Be touchy feely. Get deep and speak about the profound and intimate.

## LEARNING FROM LIVER FAILURE

A friend recently shared with me a story from a sad funeral. The man was in his early sixties and had liver failure from years of drinking too much. Outside of his liver, he was in tip-top shape. Finally, his liver gave out, resulting in his death. Everyone saw it and tried to stop it, but failed.

The sad part, however, was this man's niece. His niece, who also struggles with alcoholism, made a scene at the funeral/wake when she tried to get others to do shots in honor of her uncle. Many of the attendees refused on principle, while a few tried to encourage her to learn a lesson from her uncle's life.

My point in sharing this story is that self-deception can occur with or without our knowledge. We may be vaguely aware of the lines we repeat or we may be completely clueless. Making progress on living beautifully in friction involves seeing past our self-deception. With the niece in our story, pretty much all observers outside her head (and maybe her husband) know the niece is an alcoholic or at least think she drinks too much. The path the niece is heading down is obvious to her loved ones, but she simply cannot see it.

As we talk about some solutions below, let's assume that we all struggle to some degree with being fully honest about our path. Let's assume first that these truths are for us before we turn to help others.

## THE RULE OF WISDOM

We need wisdom in order to respond to the frictions in our lives. Wisdom is navigating the complex realities of life. Wisdom distills truth into action. To effectively deal with friction, we need to see it not as a problem to solve but as a tension to manage.

Wisdom involves less black-and-white thinking. It is asking which option is best in light of what has happened, what is happening, and what will happen.

Andy Stanley calls this the "Best Question Ever" (and his book by that name is well worth a read):

> In light of my past experience, my current situation, and my future hopes and dreams, what is the wise thing for me to do?

The language of wisdom gives us middle ground to think outside of the box. It fosters creativity. It pushes us to think. It drives us to apply knowledge well.

Wisdom takes into account our past experiences. For a mutual friend we'll call Steve, going to a bar on Friday might not be bad. But for Heather, it might be a horrible decision. Steve and Heather have different past experiences. Wisdom helps us distinguish between what is good or bad in general and what is good or bad for us.

Wisdom takes into account our current life stage. Picture the parents bringing home their third child. With young kids in formative years, working lots of nights might not be wise. For a newly minted empty nester, nights might not really mean as much. The med student who wants to get through med school should sleep well and study hard, right? But for the recent MBA grad with all the degrees they want, studying and sleep aren't as critical.

Wisdom adjusts in light of our future dreams. For those starting out in business, every penny counts. The future dream of a healthy business drives them to cut spending with joy for the one-day dream of having a significant company. To the family on vacation desiring to connect well and make memories with their kids at the beach, spending doesn't mean the same. Perhaps they need to loosen the reins a bit in order to extend the vacation by one more day, seizing valuable family time.

## LIST OPTIONS

A practical starting point to developing wisdom is listing the options. Dave Ramsey reminds us, "Options take away a lot of the fear of making the wrong choices." With bigger decisions, why not put the options down on paper and see them in black and white? We do this in business, so why not our personal life?

When you face a similar issue multiple times, or one with large consequences, try to write out at least five options. Use the rule of wisdom to choose the best. Listing out five or six options really forces us to think, pushing past either/or and allowing for a better decision-making paradigm.

This all sounds simple, but of course it's not. The rule of wisdom is easy to write but hard to follow. You may err on one side or the other. You may actively choose to lean toward one extreme in a particular situation in order to accomplish some other goal, such as building a relationship. Other times you may need to have a hard conversation because you've been taken advantage of.

Wisdom applied to daily life needs reflection and is applied uniquely.

## SEEKING WISDOM AND CLARITY

When you fight about money or overly focus on self with money, ask these questions:

- What would be the downside of delaying this?
- Based on past patterns, is this something I may regret?
- Can I easily reverse this if change my mind?
- What else could we use the money for? (This involves more options than a simple yes or no).
- If I'm not clearly hearing from God right now, should I make this decision or wait until later? (Is the timing right to make this decision now?)
- If I were to pray about this and the answer was not want I want, would I really want to hear that answer clearly? (Am I emotionally attached to this decision?)

## EVALUATION

1. With friction in your life, do you find you are aware of jumping to extremes? Where you regularly deceive yourself about the hard stuff: money, work, friends, kids, time? How about a close friend? Where do they self-deceive?

2. Was it easier to answer the last question for you or for someone else? Why do you think that is true?

3. How much are guilt and shame playing into your decision paradigm? What past decisions have you made that were motivated by these and you weren't aware of it? To what degree on a 6-point scale, 1 being low and 6 high, are you being influenced by guilt and shame in decisions?

4. When we discussed how we are often blind to our own patterns, was there a situation that kept coming back up in your mind? What are you going to do about it? What is one step that would move you closer to solving that problem?

5. How would some of your actions today change if you started concentrating on eternity?

Next, we'll discuss the role of contentment, envy, whimsy, comparison, and need in our understanding of wealth. Then we'll move into solutions for finding, maintaining, and developing authentic community in spite of the obstacles and enemies of affluence.

**Suggested Reading**

*Life Together* by Dietrich Bonhoeffer
*Daring Greatly* by Brene Brown
*Getting Naked* by Patrick Lencioni
*Principle of the Path* by Andy Stanley

# COMMUNITY FOR THE AFFLUENT

*"I can't believe God put us on this earth to be ordinary."*
- Lou Holtz -

*"It is more fun to talk with someone who doesn't use long, difficult words but rather short, easy words like 'What about lunch?'"*
- A. A. Milne, author of Winnie-the-Pooh -

*"So live that you wouldn't mind selling your pet parrot to the town gossip."*
- Will Rogers -

Picture a ship, not a little boat, but a massive oceangoing vessel. The captain just received news of a massive hurricane. The captain now has a tough decision to make. Stay in the harbor and weather the storm there, hoping to stay in the relative safety of the docks, or head out to meet the gales head on. At first one would think that staying in the docks would make more sense. However, ships aren't built to be in dock; they are built for the sea.

The ship is actually more secure when it leaves the "safety" of the docks and heads out to meet the storm head on. The ship is at more risk near the cement moorings of the docks and sea floor than crashing in the waves. The waves, however high and fierce they may be, are safer for the ship than the dock. This is much to the chagrin of the seasick sailor.

We, too, are like that storm-tossed ship. We are built for difficulty and the risk and reward of relationships, not the apparent safety of anonymity, isolation, and seclusion. We were not designed to be alone. Yet community is difficult for the affluent. But leaving a seaworthy legacy requires you have a good crew.

Let me tell you a story. I think it might resonate even if the numbers and ages are different.

## Robert and Linda Harris: A Case Study

Robert built a successful business over the last 20 years. He recently had his ever-so-popular liquidity event when he sold his company. Like many before him in small business, everything changed in that moment. Leading up to the sale, however, he lived a normal life. He had an executive salary then, but not much above his staff. Like most small business owners, he had balance sheet net worth but no cash—until the liquidity event.

When the sale happened, he said, "It wasn't too big of a deal for daily life." He went into work for several months after like nothing really happened. He still ate at the same places, drove the same car, and lived in the same house. But, little by little, the full amount of the multi-million-dollar sale dawned on him.

He planned a trip that he couldn't have taken while he was in the building years of the business. It wasn't extravagant in terms of trips by his friends' standards. After all, they had been on around-the-world trips at this point a few times, and this was he and his wife's, Linda's, first time to go.

They were introduced to how the other half lives. Affluence seemed to be a new world of customs— with a new language. They found new affluent friends and bought new wardrobes. Robert would say later that this felt like they entered a "new land of affluence, and he and Linda were immigrants." This land felt foreign, but as Robert shared, "You can get used to the perks pretty quickly . . . it seems too quickly."

As Robert and Linda adjusted, they noticed it wasn't completely easy on all parties. As they started to enjoy their money, old friends would make small comments at first. Linda's sister, Nancy, was dripping with envy when she said, "Oh, it must be nice to be able to go on those trips." Linda responded, "Well Robert and I saved for so many years, why shouldn't we enjoy a little?"

At first, they didn't do anything too big, until they planned the trip to South America. Robert thought it was best to only go on big trips once a year since they don't want to be flashy. But their Israel trip had to be rescheduled to the same year as their South America trip due to the ever-changing political environment in the Middle East.

It was again Linda's sister, Nancy, who first blew up. It may have been jealousy or maybe just a little bit of accountability. Linda had told her when the sale happened that they weren't going to change. But now with two big trips in one year, Nancy thought she was doing her sister a favor. After all, Linda had said she "wasn't going to become some country club diva." Now here she is taking another trip at the same time when Chris, her only son, was graduating college. Family has always been important, but it seems the money is getting to their heads. Nancy seemed to be comparing the details she thought she saw with what she heard Linda say back in high school.

Nancy's husband, Charlie, also noted that when Robert sold the business, he started to change. It was the small stuff like getting a lawn guy. That was something Robert said he would never do, because of how particular he was about grubs and dandelions. But Charlie now was starting to see how that lawn guy was being treated, and it felt like Robert was making others into servants.

It was fine by Charlie "if Robert wanted to treat his lawn guy as a servant, so long as Robert didn't treat him that way." But it really showed up when Robert off-handedly made a comment about Charlie's crabgrass. This happened during the Memorial Day weekend barbeque, the one where Linda brought those fancy appetizers from their Italy trip. Charlie felt like a little kid when Robert told him how to fix the crabgrass problem. Charlie told him where he could "take his advice" and stormed out of the back yard.

To Robert, Charlie's blow-up came out of nowhere. Is this what it felt like to be envied? He and Charlie had always talked about lawn care, gardening, and house maintenance. In his mind this was really a little bit of melodrama. He knew he hadn't changed since the sale, but everybody was reacting to the smallest details and comments, like if he asked what his share of the bill was when they went out to eat or if his nephew Chris was going to move off campus or stay in the dorms. Charlie and Nancy reacted as though they were being rebuked and put down for not having enough saved up in Chris's 529 accounts, or potentially trying to buy their affection one meal at a time.

What had been such a great relationship seemed to change drastically in a short period of time due to money.

Sound familiar? I've heard several variations of this story with people as they adjust to money coming in the door. It is the people you are closest to that will react the quickest. While there is no simple panacea to complex issues, let's dive headlong into a few suggestions for community for affluent folks.

## THE ROAD TO COMMUNITY

Community is different from case to case, but there are some common elements to consider. If community is the destination, then I'd like to outline the map, by showing the vehicle to community, addressing our speed of approach, and outlining some potholes along the road.

### 1. A Vehicle to Community

Who are the people that will be part of your community? These are the attributes of a faithful friend:

**A true and loving friend is Truthful.** With affluent people, truthfulness is quite hard. Very successful business owners or CEOs interact with few people who are not paid by them or pitching to get something from them. Getting a friend who will give you what you need to hear and not simply what you want to hear is rare. This level of truth is harder to find the higher up you go on the ladder of success and influence.

I recently spoke with an ultra-high-net-worth lady who shared she was done with programs and organizations. She had been hoodwinked one too many times. For true community to flourish, there needs to be honest, truthful communication. A truthful friend will tell you your zipper is down, you are being unloving to your spouse, you drink too much, or you are heading in the wrong direction. Proverbs 9:8 says, "Do not reprove a scoffer, or he will hate you; reprove a wise man, and he will love you." Wise people will take a rebuke or correction well. Fools do not. Truth is required for friendship.

**A true and loving friend is Transparent.** Transparency is being the real you without the "impress me" filter up. With real friends, you don't need to preface every bad parenting story with the "but I'm really a good parent" veneer. Transparency is rare for the affluent who feel pressure everywhere to have it all together. Polished social media posts, flattering stories, well-dressed and well-behaved kids, and timely humor are expected of the successful. But with friends, you can be real, unvarnished, plastic-wrap-free, and truly transparent. You can be fully known and fully loved.

Being fully known with warts and all is risky. Being fully known requires opening up about the not-so-great aspects of you. Being fully known in the context of loving, caring relationship is a huge comfort, but having been burned in the past makes this level of vulnerability at times painful. It is, however, hard to be fully known without transparent, vulnerable communication.

**A true and loving friend stands the test of Time.** Intimate, close-knit, deep, and lifelong friends can't happen by only attending conferences or occasional dinners or fundraising events together. There needs to be follow-up and persistent relationship. It takes time to get to know someone well enough to put something away in their fridge without having to ask or to know that person's tendency to come to a rolling stop at stop signs.

I've found that, with friends who have been willing to be truthful, who confront me on sin, call me out for being a jerk, and show me hypocrisy on hard things, we are even more wonderfully close after the risk of vulnerability. But this depth in relationship doesn't happen overnight.

**A true and loving friend is Treasured.** (Or, if you don't like my amiable attempt at alluring alliteration here and possibly prefer your points made delightfully devoid of duplicated digits, you can simply say "enjoyable"). With work, family, or civic connections, you are somewhat defined by the nature of the environment. Community and friendship, however, you get to choose. There is an enjoyment here that might not be found in the other places. To work well with someone, you can be polar opposites, and it could still be really good for your career. With community, there is fun, maybe even whimsy, enjoyment, and treasured time. You look forward to being with them.

Robert and Linda found it best to connect with couples on double dates first, two-on-two so to speak. And then their community breakthrough happened when they began to think about connecting like-minded couples together. Linda said, "I just sent an email to friends that I knew would get along—with their permission of course. I would simply say something like, 'based on our conversations, you two might get along well.' And then I'd step out to see what happened." After time, Robert and Linda have built up a network, a growing community of people they can talk with about deeper things.

Linda especially found she needed to be free from her expectations of community. She had a great group of friends from college that she constantly compared new friends to. Linda shared, "I had to remember college was such a unique season in life. For me, college was four years in which you do little else other than 'study,' a.k.a. hang out in a virtually responsibility-free environment. Friendships forged in that pivotal time are different than the rest of life. When I got over that hurdle of trying to find that type of group again, it was huge for me accepting the friendships developing around me."

> "ANSWER NOT A FOOL ACCORDING TO HIS FOLLY, LEST YOU BE LIKE HIM YOURSELF. ANSWER A FOOL ACCORDING TO HIS FOLLY, LEST HE BE WISE IN HIS OWN EYES."
>
> **PROVERBS 26:4-5**

I don't think these two sayings contradict each other. I think the point is clear: you can't win when dealing with a fool according to his folly. Or, to say it another way, attributed to George

Carlin, "Never debate with a fool, he will take you down to his level and beat you with experience."

## 2. Speed of the Journey

In Jim Collins' book, *Great by Choice*, he mentions the concept of "bullets before cannons."

Picture you are back in the olden days of ships and fighting pirates. You just have enough gunpowder for one cannonball. You start to debate whether you should fire or not fire. If we miss, it could be devastating, but if we don't try, we can't hit. Then, your indecision becomes too great and the enemy is almost upon you. Instead of thinking simply about firing versus not firing (which is that binary trap again), why not test a few bullets first before you fire your cannon? What a great way to test and see if you can get your trajectory and timing right, given the wind and the yaw of the sailboat. Bob Buford calls this idea a "low-cost probe."

Applying his principle relationally is huge. If you use this principle now, you don't need to then go from hello to spilling out your deepest darkest secrets. You don't need to go from zero to 90 in one meeting.

This is a better approach—letting relationships develop naturally. It's testing the water, so to speak. Note the level at which others share. Note whether or not they keep your information confidential. If you begin to share information, and they pour it over the Internet or gossip about you, then you don't share anything more. Glad you just tested the water as opposed to jumping off the dock, right?

Robert added on this idea, "You almost need to mirror to a

certain extent the response they give you. But you can lead with vulnerability and openness before they're going to respond with trust. It's a little bit of a chicken-and-egg dilemma." It's perfectly natural to expect the other person to reciprocate with vulnerability as well. It's not science, but more of an art.

You may find that as you've been growing in depth of relationship with somebody for a season, then they might start to pull back. Apply wisdom here. Do you pull back too? Potentially address the issue? It really depends.

Test the water; think bullets before cannons.

**3. Potholes in the Road**

It is important to understand the pothole of envy. Envy is different from admiration. Kierkegaard calls envy "unhappy admiration." Admiration has warmth. To a certain extent, those who excel will always face envy. Henry David Thoreau said, "Envy is the tax which all distinction must pay." But that doesn't mean you have to live with or accept all that comes with it.

I hear comments about envy on a consistent basis. Oftentimes people believe you are more well-off than you are. I keep this axiom on my tongue frequently, "What Peter says about Paul says more about Peter than about Paul." When someone judges you, speaks ill of you, or is just mean, I find it key to remember that what they showed doesn't reveal as much about me as it does about them.

The guiding principle here is to be at peace with all men. Envy and jealousy from others is ridiculously common and not regularly talked about.

## SOME HELP TO REDUCE ENVY'S POWER IN RELATIONSHIPS

1. Think in terms of empathy, not pity. Empathy is being able to put yourself in others' shoes. It's a fabulous skill to learn. Pity makes people small. It's quite sad, really, when others are caught up in your success. Take pity out and put empathy in. The truth is, those who are envious and jealous all the time are living a lonely existence.

2. Be wise with what you share. Appropriate distance is the key here. If you're talking with someone less affluent, beware of giving details about the recent vacation or the new car. This can be especially true in family situations.

3. Don't be falsely modest. It's nice to be affluent. Don't act like it isn't. But be aware that others will assume it's nice to have what you have. Don't underplay your situation. People see through that, and it actually exacerbates the situation.

4. Emphasize luck and gratitude. Most of us who are affluent did not get there completely from our skill. Luck does play a role. The timing of your success and the people it took to make it happen were not completely in your control. Even Bill Gates' success through his passion for computers would be completely different if he were born today, right? Acknowledge that you didn't directly earn everything you've been given.

5. Display an appropriate weakness. Don't always feel like you have to lead from strength. It is okay to say, "I don't have everything all figured out."

6. Get distance. Be aware of how deep you go with some people. Trust needs to be earned. Guard your distance with people appropriately.

Just be cautious about what you share about your affluence and how deep you go in a conversation. You don't always have to go to an intimate place, like discussing money or sex or your feelings. Be guarded about some issues with certain people. You can be distant in an appropriate way if you're picking up signals of envy.

7. Confront, if necessary. Be aware that if someone is new to affluence, awkward dynamics do come up. It's okay to try to clear the air and be at peace. We don't have to agree with everyone or be fighting all the time. Think through with wisdom.

The problems associated with envy and jealousy are really relationship difficulties. And they are very complex. I wish I could just say, "Do these seven things and your problems are solved." But hard problems aren't solved by simple solutions. The bottom line is that keeping the peace with everyone might not happen. But being careful with what you share and with whom you share is ultimately a matter of wisdom.

## 4. Find Contentment

We spoke about contentment in the context of our kids. The appreciate-expect-demand curve applies to us as well. Contentment is an issue of focus and will.

If we allow the Madison Avenue marketing people to focus our attention on what we don't have, then we will remarkably discontented. Richard L. Evans said, "May we never let the things we can't have or don't have or shouldn't have spoil our enjoyment of the things we do have and can have. As we value our happiness, let us not forget it. One of the greatest lessons in life is learning to be happy without the things we cannot or should not have."

Remember the movie *White Christmas* starring Bing Crosby, Danny Kaye, Rosemary Clooney, and Judy Haynes? It's Christmas classic in my house. Bing sings an old hymn that says, "Count your blessings . . . instead of sheep." I just heard it in my head sung by the man, Bing, himself. That is good advice.

In his superb book *How to Win over Worry*, Dr. John Edmund Haggai challenges us on this line of thinking, "For how much would you sell the health that God has given to you? How much does your wife's love mean to you? For what amount would you sell your reputation if it could be put on the open market?" Spend some time actually writing out your blessings. That is one way to count your blessings that will change things!

Let's think back to our friends Robert and Linda. This is an exercise they found helpful. I'd challenge you to actually fill this out. I've found no formula of how to do this to satisfy all my engineering and accounting friends. So, make it work for you.

To make it easier, don't worry about inflation. Use your actual resources, or ones you could or would get, if the situation happened.

Imagine each item as happening in a vacuum separate from the other events/questions. Write in an actual dollar amount next to each one. Quantify, as close to possible, these blessings we often take for granted. It might be helpful to think in categories: Whatever it takes, $1M plus, $100k-$1M, and under $100k.

- If you were stuck in the 1700s, how much would you pay for a modern bathroom? Toilet? Cosmetics? Soft tissue paper when you have a cold? A dentist to get rid of tooth pain?
- What amount of money would you take in trade for your professional connections and your network? Your resume or CV experiences? Lesson learned from failure?
- For me, if shipping and grocery industries didn't exist, I would never have experienced the wonder of a mango or coconut. What would you pay if living in 1776 to experience bananas, grapes, mangoes, and the like?
- What price would you pay to have electricity and all the gadgets and benefits with it today if living in 1880?
- Imagine your sex life didn't exist at all. How much would you pay to be able to have passionate, soul-touching sex regularly with your spouse?
- How much would you pay to know how to read if you couldn't?
- If living in Hitler's Germany or an equivalent situation, how much money would you spend to end his regime or get out from under it?
- Imagine your kids were just kidnapped. What price would you pay to save your children (and/or grandchildren, nieces, or nephews) from danger?
- What do you highly value that we didn't include on this list?

Take a few minutes and write out an answer to each question.

Estimate a value to the blessings in your life. What blessings indeed we possess! I think these numbers show us more than our simple net worth. Non-balance-sheet assets are deeper and far more meaningful.

I used to think that being content would destroy my drive and ambition. I've found that not to be true. If I strive to stay grateful, that doesn't impact my drive. In fact, what I've found is that gratitude and contentment really allow me to enjoy the ambitious and adventurous ride. You can still have drive and ambition. Pausing for a moment to be grateful or write a thank you note helps you enjoy the journey.

Question: Who do you think understands being sober better, the inebriated person or the sober one? I would say the inebriated person understands slowed thinking and slurred speech, but doesn't comprehend sobriety and its difference to their current state. The sober person can more fully grasp the effects of alcohol, comparing it with his rational state of mind. Likewise, people in pain understand only pain. They don't fully comprehend healing and all that goes with restoration and recovery. There is a certain point with deep pain where we only know pain. Healing gives perspective on the past and can allow you to change our view.

If you are drunk with ambition, you don't understand contentment in its proper setting. Contentment is found not with any monetary amount. It comes with self-control and discipline.

### 3. Watch Out for Emotions

There is no universal pain point to draw awareness to friendships. If you are trying to lose weight or are completely unaware of your current weight gain, there can be really obvious pain points on the journey. There will be looks of disgust that will really make you aware or a comment from someone or a pinch to your stomach. Trying to wear a pair of pants that don't fit. There are pain points with weight. What are the pain points with relationships?

Emotions can act as signals for relational pain points. Watch out for emotions like anger, sadness, loneliness, shame, hurt, fear, guilt, and gladness. Emotional awareness is a crucial skill you need to learn to dive deeply into relationships.

As a man, this didn't come naturally to me, and it still doesn't. Guys, let's be honest. Ladies typically are better than we are on these heart-level issues. But that also makes us pause a bit more to understand the "soft stuff." I would strongly encourage you to figure out how to figure yourself out. Understanding the role of emotions in yourself but also the people around you that you care about is big stuff.

The best analogy I've found with emotions is to picture emotions as the central nervous system of the body. The pain of an emotion raises awareness to the heart-level issue that needs to be addressed. I recently broke my tailbone. It was very painful to sit. Every time I sat down on it wrong, pain shot through my whole body, as if to say, "Hey there's a problem here. Help us out." This is true emotionally as well. When you find yourself experiencing powerful or unknown emotions in an area, that's a message telling you, "Hey, pay attention here. We need some help!"

## 4. Showing Need

I've found I help people I enjoy and meet the needs of people I like. But is that the full story? Did the affection come first, or the meeting needs? In reality, we increase affections when we do favors and help people. We may start out liking them, but our affection grows even more after we help them or do them a favor. This principle is called reciprocity. It is one reason we love our kids so much. We've helped them out at all hours of the night.

But what needs do affluent people have? Or better yet, what needs can they share? Sometimes they aren't even aware of their own needs.

There is a powerful scene in the movie Family Man starring Nicolas Cage, from back in 2000. The premise of the movie starts in this scene. Jack, Nicolas Cage's character, is an uber-successful Manhattan businessman. He has the large condo downtown with a bellman, a prestigious job, expensive suits, fast cars, and all the trappings to go with them. While walking home from work, he encounters a man he tries to help.

Jack: Well, everybody needs something.

Cash: Well, what do you need Jack?

Jack: Me?

Cash: You just said, everybody needs something.

Jack: I got everything I need.

Cash: Wow. It must be great being you.

The movie then continues to give Jack a glimpse of the road he didn't travel, where he is a family man (thus the name of the movie). It calls me back to what matters. It's a modernized It's a Wonderful Life, to a certain extent. It is definitely worth a watch if you're wrestling witvh relationships and wealth.

We talked in Chapter Six about the wealthy man getting his garage fixed. There is an attitude that if you can afford to pay someone to fix it, then you don't need to call the friends to help. The built-in community around need is missing from the affluent.

Look at the difference, then, with this wealthy guy and someone with fewer resources. The poor man sees hours of hang-out time and connection. The principle of reciprocity would say those friends now like him even more because they helped him out.

But the wealthy guy calls some companies to get quotes. He is afraid, due to the size of his house, that he is going to be taken advantage of by the estimates. He gets three quotes and picks the middle one. He tells them what to do. When they are working, he pays attention to one detail to make sure they will work hard, since he is "paying attention" and "inspecting their work." Chances are, he may really have no idea how the work should be done. Then, he pays the bill with little interaction with another human as a human. He can end up treating all people involved as a means to an end. They fix his problem. This can quickly turn into an "I-it" relationships.

When we look at people as part of what Martin Buber calls an "I-it" relationship, we start to see people as a means to an end. This is in contrast to "I-You" relationships. In an "I-You" relationship, you see others as humans with feelings, connections, family, and dreams.

When you start thinking of some people as "it," it becomes easier to move more and more people into the category. Once you treat your server, secretary, intern, or lawn guy as an impersonal "it," then it is easier to move others into that realm as well. Watch out.

To fight "I-it" relationships, look the person in the eye, pause before you respond, listen instead of thinking about your answer, don't repeat conversations with a similar person (as in, this is the conversation I have with Starbucks baristas or my massage therapist), be okay with silence, and focus on being fully present.

According to Oxford Dictionary, empathy is "the ability to understand and share the feelings of another."[23] It's putting yourself into their shoes. Try doing that next time you head into "I-it" territory. Don't simply say—they aren't like me because they didn't work hard, or they are lazy, or they are not as smart, or they have a boring job. Really try to see things from their point of view. Understand what makes them tick. You'll be surprised at what you find.

**5. Go on a Caper**

Be adventurous and solve a need together. Bob Goff has a really fun concept that I love. In his book *Love Does*, he tells stories about capers and whimsy. I know in my life I could use some more whimsy. A caper is a fun, often spontaneous journey that will one day be a good story to tell. Shared memory is a really good building block of community.

Solve a project together (but be careful not to treat people as projects). Go on mission together to solve a common concern in your community. Instead of complaining about something, take a small step of action.

Fund some need together. It's amazing how much unity is found in doing these ventures with like-minded people. It is inspiring, fun, and great bonding like nothing else I've done.

In Portland, Oregon, there are great examples of churches and business coming together with government organizations to solve problems like poverty, illiteracy, and other huge issues around the city. There is power in working across these lines, and it's amazing how much more effective it is when it's done together, without each group setting up its own little fiefdom.

Kevin Palau, a Republican and Evangelical Christian, and Sam Adams, Democratic mayor of Portland who is openly gay, have established an interesting friendship. By all accounts, they would normally have very little to do with each other and very little in common. Yet they are helping to lead a movement in Portland to fight illiteracy. If you are interested, watch the YouTube video called, "When a Gay Mayor Partners with Evangelical Churches in Portland." Their caper brought unity.

My friend Tim Mohns is a financial planner in the Chicagoland area from whom I learned a great deal on these issues during long lunches. He tells stories of engaging with certain clients on these journeys of building orphanages, digging wells, and helping where there is need. He funds some, and the client or clients fund some. What a fun idea! Tim shared that after a while, the joy from generous giving together is all they talk about in meetings. That would change the financial planning conversation to something totally different.

This could also look like starting an orphanage in the Dominican Republic instead of buying a second or third home. This could be offering a matching gift for year-end for your second-favorite charity. Maybe you could find a big evil you want to end and gather some folks to start to end it with you.

### 6. Stop Comparing

*"Envy is ever joined with the comparing of a man's self; and where there is no comparison, no envy."* —Sir Francis Bacon

In going through life, my brothers had a very different experience than me with money. I was younger when a lot of the big financial changes happened, and as a result I felt it very differently. Even though my brothers and I had very similar situations and the very same parents, our experiences were not identical. If I compare myself to them or they to me, it's not fair. And let's be honest, is there any win comparing? What good can come of it? One man I interviewed wisely said, "We don't make any friends by bragging about anything, especially when it comes to our kids."

My brother Jeff runs an auto repossession business or more commonly called, a "repo company." He jokingly says that he steals cars for a living. There is not one neighborhood from Detroit to Chicago to Indianapolis from which he doesn't repossess cars. He says it's routine to find bigger homes he visits to repo cars outfitted with sheets on the hidden back windows and pricey wood blinds on the front ones that are visible from the road.

I'm told that in bigger cities and trendy areas there are several companies that rent out furniture, even decorations, in addition to catering, so people can appear to be better off to their party guests. Keep that in mind when you are attending a society event. You might not have all the facts.

Nostalgia is a weird form of comparison too. Nostalgia is living in the glory days when we had . . . or we didn't have. What good comes when you compare the current days in light of the olden days? Nostalgia has a place. Remembering has its place. But nostalgia's rose-colored glasses often don't help you live today. I'm not sure about you, but for me, nostalgia has a great ability to edit my memory. When I look back, the glasses of nostalgia have edited greatly, and I'm fondly remembering a time that really didn't exist. Watch out for nostalgia's ability to edit and change the memory.

Recalling the days when kids could ride bikes without helmets, Pluto was a planet, the only seat belts were a mother's arm, and ice cream could be bought for whatever price doesn't help you live today. It is tempting to look back and live there. But remembering well is not easily done. Don't get me wrong, I'm all for history and learning from the past. I love pouring over old books and History Channel shows. But living there is not a good option. You are meant for this day, this time, and this moment.

What if we stop measuring up, showing off, attempting to keep up and fit in? Let's leave behind petty games and trivial measurements. Let's be real, honest, and open. What if we started with us and didn't focus on them?

Let's instead be grateful for what we have. Let's move our

hearts into gratitude and thanksgiving. Let's stop pretending to live in Camelot. Let's find people we can trust, let our guard down, and do life with those who matter to us.

A poignant scene from the Velveteen Rabbit has always made this point incredibly well. Remember that little rabbit? He wants to be loved and real. Sound familiar? I hope you hear it differently in light of the conversation we've had here.

> "Real isn't how you are made," said the Skin Horse. "It's a thing that happens to you. When a child loves you for a long, long time, not just to play with, but REALLY loves you, then you become Real."
> "Does it hurt?" asked the Rabbit.
> "Sometimes," said the Skin Horse, for he was always truthful. "When you are Real you don't mind being hurt."
> "Does it happen all at once, like being wound up," he asked, "or bit by bit?"
> "It doesn't happen all at once," said the Skin Horse. "You become. It takes a long time. That's why it doesn't happen often to people who break easily, or have sharp edges, or who have to be carefully kept. Generally, by the time you are Real, most of your hair has been loved off, and your eyes drop out and you get loose in the joints and very shabby. But these things don't matter at all, because once you are Real you can't be ugly, except to people who don't understand."

"…because once you are Real you can't be ugly, except to people who don't understand." Let that point sink in. When someone who doesn't understand you speaks, filter those words well. When others are critical, remember their words reveal more about them than it does you. Rather than letting others' comments be a barrier to building community, make the choice to invest in others. If you want to matter at what matters, you have to show up and lean in.

**EVALUATION**

1. Do you ever feel lonely? What can you do to feel less lonely?
2. Do you agree community is important for the affluent? If so, what are the barriers to community that you have encountered?
3. Can you make a short list of several people you think you could cultivate to build your community? If so, what's stopping you?
4. How many people in your life do you truly trust? How many of your friends would put you on their list?
5. Write out the top areas where you are tempted to compare. Then actively try to remember to avoid them. With each area, try to find a signal thought or emotion that will help you will recognize when you are moving into unhealthy comparison.

## Suggested Reading

*Your Life… Well Spent* by Russ Crosson
*Great by Choice* by Jim Collins
*When Helping Hurts* by Steve Corbett and Brian Fikkert
*Love Does* by Bob Goff
*Daring Greatly* by Brene Brown
*unHeritage* by Tom Conway, Steve Gardner, Bill High, Jerry Nuerge, and Ryan Zeeb

# EPILOGUE

By now, it should be easy to see that I don't claim to have all the answers on wealth and wealth management. There are plenty of books that claim to provide one easy answer that will revolutionize your thinking and change your life.

My aims here have been more modest. First, I've tried to name many of the forces that serve to make the flip side of affluence difficult to navigate for both the newly wealthy and those who have received substantial inheritances. There's value, I believe, in simply describing these experiences so that you can reflect on their presence in your own life.

Second, I've tried to offer some potential solutions and "best practices" to the challenges faced by the affluence, especially in the areas of relationships and parenting. Again, these are not one-size-fits-all, and no one solution is the be-all-and-end-all. But if you apply some of the principles and lessons in this book in small ways over time, I believe you'll see a real difference in your own confidence, spending habits, wealth management, and overall contentment.

Ultimately, I hope this book has also served to point you to Jesus, the One who can heal all our sorrows and usher us into a new understanding of both ourselves and others. The principles in the Bible are timeless; you don't have to be a Christian to appreciate their wisdom. But anything short of knowing Jesus directly is only a substitute for what really matters. That's why I hope this book has made you think more about living in light of your legacy, not just during your lifetime but into eternity.

The most dangerous word in all of this is not what you would think. It's not "no." The most dangerous word is "later." Postponing change for another time is the biggest challenge in living a life of significance. I would encourage you to write down one thing you want to change. Tell someone and make a step toward implementing that one change today. Not tomorrow, or the next day—let today be your day of action. Go pursue significance!

## APPENDIX A
# THE FAITH DILEMMA

*"What comes into our minds when we think about God is the most important thing about us."*
- A. W. Tozer -

*"Never be afraid to trust an unknown future to a known God."*
- Corrie ten Boom -

*"All I have seen teaches me to trust the Creator for all I have not seen."*
- Ralph Waldo Emerson -

If Jesus isn't your deal, I'm really glad you are here. For the most part, I wrote this book for you. But I'm sure along the way what I've said about the Bible and Jesus has made you pause or even frustrated you. (And chances are if someone gave you this book, they may have been a little too excited to have you read this appendix). How we handle money has many spiritual implications, so I couldn't leave this part unsaid.

If I can be honest, one of my biggest struggles in writing this book, as a Christian, is I feel that I may have sold you short thus far with my solutions. From what I can tell, in order for life to be lived to the fullest and best, it has to be under the banner of a relationship with Jesus. He designed us for him. But I'm not trying to be preachy. I want to spend a few minutes outlining one thought that I hope will put in perspective why I think Jesus is such a big deal and potentially why faith might become a big issue as you've become more affluent.

Picture a young career-aged man named Jack. He is dressed in a suit, neat shoes, and a sensible tie. He has been working for a great company in his area of passion and has been doing so since straight out of school. He has been at the company for four years, and he is sitting outside of his boss's office.

He thinks he is going to get promoted. Everything and everyone in the company so far tells him that is the case. Whatever they have put in his hands has truly succeeded. He is not married and not really interested in marriage. To him, marriage means less time with his friends, less money to buy what he wants, and, in general, less freedom.

If you were to explain marriage to him and try to sell him on the institution of it, he'd not be interested. It's for others. He has seen it not work out, but some of his friends have tried it and liked it. Marriage just isn't for him. He often says in a sing-song voice, "Good for you if that is your cup of tea, but marriage truly is just not for me."

Jack wants to live how he wants to live and not let any ancient ideas of love stop him from living life his way. Marriage is an "it," a concept. For him, marriage is academic. He has reasons why marriage is not his deal; he has even run the numbers and has spreadsheets as to why it is not a good idea. He has his objections all laid out.

But what happens to Jack's view of marriage when *she* walks into his life? Then it's a different story.

What happens when Jack meets the one woman who just knocks him off his feet? Then the objections and spreadsheets start to matter less and less. It's not that he has all his answers figured out, but that marriage starts to look real for him in his future. Because then, marriage was about it, the concept. Now, marriage is about *her*, the girl.

From what I have seen, this is how most adults who don't know Jesus tend to think about him. Most people examine the claims about the Bible from an academic perspective. Jesus, to them, is a concept or an idea. Sure, some of the stuff Jesus said is nice, "I like that love your neighbor bit." But like Jack may say, "Good for you if that is your cup of tea, but that Jesus stuff is just not for me." For many, they have reasons and objections as to why it is not their deal.

But what happens when God walks into their life in a personal way? Then it's a different story.

Then something happens they can't explain. Suddenly, the objections start to matter less and less. Suddenly, it's about him, not about it. Suddenly, they are brought face to face with the idea that God came to save them personally. Jesus, who made the world, died on the cross, and rose again is not an academic lecture from college, but rather a person they have experienced. Then it is a different story.

For you who have not seen God show up personally, I understand. You have your reasons. You may have a good friend who goes to church, and you think it is fine for her but not for you. I would suggest that if you are open to God being real, why not talk to him? If he's not real, then nothing you say will matter anyway. But ask God to show up and be real to you. What can it hurt?

What happens next might not be flashing lights, a dream, or something drastic. But changes most likely will start, or, quite possibly, changes have already started to happen.

If you are not willing to ask God to show up, why not? What about God showing up makes you pause? Does God showing up mean you'd have to change how you live? Yes, most likely it does. But hear me now. What happens if you are wrong and the Bible is right? If God is real and the Bible is true, are you ready to be wrong? Eternity is not short.

You may say, "Do you think you can talk me into being a Christian in so short a time?" No, I don't. Unless God is moving in your life, these words are but another thing you'll joke about or ignore. But if God has been working in your life in ways that don't fully make sense under any other premise, then this might be the final straw. God might supernaturally use words on a page to change and alter the course of your life.

You may also say, "But I still have my objections!" You do, and I don't want to minimize those. I'm sure if we sat down and talked, your reasons would be real, your experiences would be completely legit, and you would make total sense. If I can press you a little, where have you looked for answers to those

## APPENDIX A

issues? Have you read any good books from a Christian who addresses your objections? And why does this issue raise such emotions and sometimes anger in you? Why is the name Jesus so different?

If you have objections, then let me suggest some resources for some of the common issues at the end of this chapter. But allow me to address two common objections first. One is the hypocrites in the church and the other is being burned by past experiences.

**1. What About Hypocrites?**

You may say, "But there are hypocrites in the church!" And oh, there are. And I probably can name more than you can. Two things on hypocrites:

One, hypocrites don't change the message; they just make it harder to hear. There are hypocrites and posers at the gym, but I still need to work out. There are posers at my favorite sporting events, but I still go. The people do, unfortunately, make it hard to listen sometimes, but the truth of the gospel message is still there.

Two (and more importantly), I'm a hypocrite. I fail spiritually a lot. I've messed up tons. But when you think about it, hypocrites and failures in the church make me think I can be there, too. In fact, the Bible suggests that we're all hypocrites in one way or another.

When I read the Bible about saints who didn't finish well or really mess up big, then that makes me feel like I can be at home there. Moses, David, Peter, and Paul all did some really big things for God. But they are also really messed up. Moses killed a man. David committed adultery and covered it up with murder. Peter helped found the church, but he denied being connected to Jesus three times in one night at a very pivotal time and constantly stuck his foot in his mouth. The Apostle Paul held the coats of people and watched with affirmation as someone was killed for following Jesus. Paul also sought to destroy the church before God showed up to be real in his life.

Yes, there are hypocrites in the church, but that makes me feel like I fit in. I lie to make myself look better, yet I lose my temper at my kids. I forget daily about why I'm here, struggle with being lazy, and at the same time I work too much. I am nowhere near where I want to be. But I'm moving. I am trying to change and move forward and be more like the man I want to be. I believe that is most possible when I trust God for help and guidance.

**2. But I was Burned in the Local Church**

Me too. I hear you on this one. I can tell you, the deepest wounds in my life were experienced in settings where I was supposed to be loved and cared for. Those pains hurt deeply. Let me challenge you. Are you living in light of the pain or the solution? Is that the real reason you aren't following Jesus or simply an excuse to live how you want to live? I know I'm pushing into areas I don't know about and also areas you may not have talked to many people about. But please hear my heart on this issue. There is hope. There is healing. There is a place where you can be known and be loved without fear or hiding.

If you are hurt and currently in the middle of pain, please

forgive me. I don't mean for my tone here to sound cavalier. If we were sitting knee to knee, I would listen, and try not to talk. If you are in the middle of pain—find healing. Deciding big stuff like faith and the rest of the issues we talk through in this book in pain is like running a race with a monkey on your back. First, get healing from the pain. Get the monkey off your back. Then get back in the race.

G.K. Chesterton says, "The Christian ideal has not been tried and found wanting; it has been found difficult and left untried."

## REFRAMING YOUR PERSPECTIVE

Let me attempt to reframe your perspective on faith. For those of you who still have a simplistic faith from a bad experience in church or a college professor who popped your little bubble, let me allow Sally Lloyd-Jones to help reframe the discussion and the Bible in your mind. This is from her excellent work, *The Story of God's Love for You*.

> Now, some people think the Bible is a book of rules, telling you what you should and shouldn't do. The Bible certainly does have some rules in it. They show you how life works best. But the Bible isn't mainly about you and what you should be doing. It's about God and what he has done.
>
> Other people think the Bible is a book of heroes, showing people you should copy. The Bible does have some heroes in it, but (as you'll soon find out) most of the people in the Bible aren't heroes at all. They make some big mistakes (sometimes on purpose). They get afraid and run away. At times they are downright mean.

No, the Bible isn't a book of rules, or a book or heroes. The Bible is most of all a Story. It's an adventure story about a young Hero who comes from a far country to win back his lost treasure. It's a love story about a brave Prince who leaves his palace, his throne—everything—to rescue the ones he loves. It's like the most wonderful of fairy tales that has come true in real life!

You seem the best thing about this Story is—it's true.

## THE DRAGON IN US

One of the books in C. S. Lewis' great series The Chronicles of Narnia has a great section I want you to hear. It's from the book *Voyage of the Dawn Treader*. It shows us a vivid picture of what faith could look like for you.

Eustace Scrub is a spoiled little boy whom no one likes and who honestly somewhat deserves his horrid name. In his greed, he seeks out a treasure and magically turns into a fire-breathing dragon. He comes to a point in the story where he only wants to be a boy again. He strives on his own strength to rid himself of the scales, scratching off layer upon layer to no avail. But Aslan, the lion who most resembles Christ in the books, comes to assist in removing the painful scales. The prototype of Jesus was able to scratch down deeper. The book describes it this way:

"The very first tear he made was so deep that I thought it had gone right into my heart. And when he began pulling the skin off, it hurt worse than anything I've ever felt. The only thing that made me able to bear it was just the pleasure of feeling the stuff peel off...

...Then he caught hold of me—I didn't like that much for

I was very tender underneath now that I'd no skin on—and threw me into the water. It smarted like anything but only for a moment. After that it became perfectly delicious and as soon as I started swimming and splashing I found that all the pain had gone from my arm. And then I saw why. I'd turned into a boy again…

After a bit the lion took me out and dressed me…in new clothes."

This is what we need. Our deepest spiritual need is to have the God who is real restore us and heal our deepest pain. We need to repent and surrender to the Lion of Judah and find Jesus as our savior. We need him to rip off our old self with its scales and pain, cleanse us, and dress us in new clothes. This is actually true for all of us, whether we have been claiming the name of Christ since childhood or are just now opening up to the movement of his Spirit.

If you are ready to make that commitment and surrender to Jesus, take a moment now and seal the deal. Pray to Him asking for forgiveness and healing. Repent of your sin and ask him to guide your life. Follow up by getting involved with a Christian community, whether that means attending the local church or setting up a meeting with a pastor.

If you are not ready to surrender to Jesus yet, let me give you resources that I have found very helpful.

## INTRODUCTORY YET NOT SIMPLISTIC

**OPTION A**—If you have objections, try *Who Made God?: And Answers to Over 100 Other Tough Questions of Faith,* edited by Norman Geisler and Ravi Zacharias.

If you've not read anything else on the topic, this is a good place to start. This book is a basic reference-like book that will cover 100 questions about faith written by some really smart people who have spent a lot of time thinking about these issues. They boil down their ideas into a page or two responses.

One of the editors of that book has some other resources too. Ravi Zacharias has a teaching podcast and radio program called "Let my people think" and "Just Thinking." He explains things very well, he is funny at times, and I love his accent.

**OPTION B**—If you are not very familiar with Christianity or its claims, try *Mere Christianity* by C. S. Lewis. It is the intro book that I still love more than any other of his many works. It is very well written and timely even years after its original publication date.

The description of the Bible we quoted early by Sally Lloyd-Jones in her book *The Story of God's Love for You* is fabulous as well. If you have a version of faith that is from your childhood or a professor in college, read this. She tells the story of the Bible in a way that will reframe the conversation. The rest of the book she wrote is equally as profound. The kid's version has the same text (or at least very similar) but has beautiful pictures. If you have kids, I can't speak highly enough of this resource. It is called *The Jesus Storybook Bible: Every Story Whispers His Name.*

**OPTION C**—If you have a Bible but have never read it, try revisiting Proverbs for its teachings about wisdom. The book of James is in the New Testament and another good source of wise

# APPENDIX A

thinking. Jesus himself can be found in all four gospels. I'd start with Mark; it's the shortest and most direct.

**OPTION D**—If you are looking for a good church that will teach the Bible and the historic Christian faith, I'd start with "The Gospel Coalition" or "The Willow Creek Association." They both are a body of churches that share resources and, from my experiences, love people well.

**OPTION E**—If you are more of an audio person, check out Andy Stanley, Tim Keller, or Chip Ingram. These are my favorite three voices in the Christian pastor world for people who are not connected with Jesus.

Andy Stanley is a fabulous leader and communicator. He phrases things well, speaking to the heart, and his words are easy to apply. The line of thinking in this chapter is influenced by his sermon series, "It's Personal." His other sermons that I've mentioned or hinted at in the book are "How to be Rich," "Principle of the Path," "Just Ask it," and "Starting Over." You can find Andy Stanley on podcasts under the name "Your move" and "Andy Stanley's Leadership podcast."

Tim Keller is a brilliant thinker and pastor out of Manhattan at Redeemer Presbyterian Church. He is very well read, academically sound, and quite articulate. If you tend to think Christianity and being smart aren't compatible, you need to check out his materials. His sermons and books are thick with rich content and insight. You can find him by searching for his church website or his books, "anywhere books are sold."

Chip Ingram is just plain real and at times raw in a way

231

that makes you love him and want to hear more. His series called "Contentment" relates to our discussion here. Or, you could start with his series, "True Spirituality," "Good to Great in God's Eyes," or "Finding God When You Need Him Most." His "Living on the Edge" podcast or radio show has great content.

**Great Reads and My Favorites**

If you are a little more advanced in your inquiry, here are a few other books I've found very helpful for clarifying what Christianity is all about:

- J. Warner Wallace, *Cold-Case Christianity: A Homicide Detective Investigates the Claims of the Gospels*
- A.W. Tozer, *Knowledge of the Holy*
- Ravi Zacharias, *The Grand Weaver: How God Shapes Us through the Events of Our Lives*
- Tim Keller, *The Reason for God: Belief in an Age of Skepticism*
- Chuck Colson and Nancy Pearson, *How Now Shall We Live?*
- Francis Chan, *Crazy Love*
- Wayne Grudem wrote a fantastic book called *Systematic Theology*; it's a deep dive, but readable. He and his son Elliot also wrote a shorter version called *Christian Beliefs: Twenty Basics Every Christian Should Know*. Both are excellent and still somewhat accessible. They are substantial! Each sentence I find wanting to read a few times to get the full depth.

**Issue-focused Online Resources**

If you have one issue that you're wrestling with and desire a longer answer, consider these online resources. They should help point you in a good direction.

- **http://www.rzim.org/bibliography/** Ravi Zacharias' site has an extensive list.
- **http://www.reasonablefaith.org/** William Lane Craig has some really good resources, even for kids.
- **http://www.breakpoint.org/resources** Chuck Colson's former organization is strong.
- **http://www.jpmoreland.com/jps-library/library/** J. P. Moreland has great content.

My seminary alma mater, Trinity Evangelical Divinity School, has one-week classes in the summer and extension courses as well that will help you dive into issues in a way that will provide some great solutions. I would recommend their systematic theology program for those who want to engage more extensively. Just search for its distance learning program.

## FINDING PEOPLE TO TALK TO

I can't stress too much the importance of having a person who can talk you through these issues. There are conferences, lectures, and videos by the authors above, so I encourage you to check them out. At the conferences, you might meet someone who can help you find more answers and come alongside you as you examine the subjects. You might also get some recommendations from local pastors, professors, friends, or family.

**FINAL WORD**

Know that there is hope; there always is and always will be. God is not silent, and he will be found if you begin looking.

I trust in this short appendix I haven't lost the effectiveness I hope to have established in the earlier chapters. Yes, I think there are answers to the questions you have. Beyond answers, I would love you to live life to its fullest. I would love you to step into a meaningful life. That life, I believe, can only be found in Jesus Christ, lived with the Bible as a guide. You'll notice that I often used Bible verses to support my points, and some people see the Bible and run the other way! But why is that? The Bible has been used as authoritative, time-tested teaching for generations of people. Even if you don't yet believe the Bible is the inspired Word of God, I encourage you to take its wisdom at face value. My aim in using these verses hasn't been to lord them over your head, but to point out how they lead to a deeper and richer life, one lived in light of eternity.

Thanks for journeying with me on these weighty matters. I know I enjoyed it. Let's go further up and further in! Journey well, my friends.

APPENDIX B
# WRITING YOUR FAMILY LEGACY STORY A.K.A. CLARIFYING THE SEAWORTHY LEGACY

I want to challenge us to apply our skill and some of our business acumen to our most important organization—our family. Many of us do very well and have had years of training to excel in business. Now I want to turn some of that onto our family structure.

Several years back, I read a simple book called Family ID. The authors, Greg Gunn and Craig Groeschel, introduced me to the idea of being purposeful and intentional about how I was leading my family. Their basic premise is that if you have a mission statement and vision for your business, then why don't you have anything for your family? That thought rocked my world.

Each year in my career, I have set up annual goals; I have a vision and mission statements. They have been wonderfully helpful. But why not have a family mission's statement and list of values, or a story? I had no answer.

More recently, I read Patrick Lencioni's The Three Big Questions for a Frantic Family. This is also a fabulous resource to press deeper into the ideas I'm touching on here.

After reading these books, I began a journey with my family that I would recommend for you as well. Start figuring out, together, how to live more purposefully. What values and principles do I want to pass down? What are the key principles and values I want for my family, and how do I get this done? The answers in this section will form the backbone of your family legacy.

Note the journey to the final project is as important to the final project itself. I'd recommend involving the age-appropriate kids, prayer, trusted friends and advisors, and a good deal of dedicated time to this endeavor.

Here are some simple steps to follow:

1) Start. As in, just do something. Jon Acuff, in his book *Start: Punch Fear in the Face, Escape Average, and Do Work that Matters*, says the only line you can control is the starting line (as a side note, that may be the coolest book title ever). So, gear up and start the process. Why not now?

2) Put pencil to paper. There is power is pushing something out your fingertips. Try it. You will be forced to define what you mean. Writing also gives a level of seriousness and commitment that really is good.

3) Think in light of principles and values. Picture a tree. Principles are who we are. They are the roots of the tree. Values are what we do. They form the trunk of the tree. The result is

the legacy we leave. That's the leaves and the fruit.

The principles are the character traits that don't change, that you want to have when you are 65 and that you want your kids to have when they are 16. Examples of my family principles are: Whimsy, Fantastic Generosity, and Dependence on Jesus.

Patrick Lencioni calls these principles "core values." He gives some good guidelines on them. One, they are not aspirational values, what you wish were true of your family. Instead, they are the essence of the family's identity—things that are true but that we want to emphasize more. Two, some good things you want to put on the list are what he calls, "permission-to-play." For instance integrity, honesty, and "others first" are good things but usually are not the main or core thing. They are more values that we have and that need to be present in order to for us function well as a family unit.

Values, then, are developed out of the unchanging principles. Right now my family values include family game nights, bacon, shared mealtimes, "give, save, spend" for our kids' allowances, the wonderful game "Socks Alive," homework before playing, "Rock, Paper, Scissors" tournaments, paper airplane competitions, annual family vacations, and more.

I know you are wondering, so let me explain. The game "Socks Alive" (which came from the book *Family ID*) is one of our family night games where they are two rules: 1) Keep your socks on. 2) Stay alive. Basically, it boils down to a big family wrestling match with tickling, taped soccer-length socks, and loads of laughter. There is a season to this one. I probably won't want to play too much when I'm in my nineties. That is why "Socks Alive" is a value but "Whimsy/Fun" is a principle.

4) Give ownership to the family. You can't simply write it down and lecture on this. The process of forming the principles is as important as the final project. Patrick Lencioni says, "Where there is no weighing in, there is no buying in." Getting your kids' input doesn't mean you are running a democracy but that you are making them feel like they are a part of the family. You are better able to understand what is best for the family when you actually take time to listen and invite their perspective. Ask questions such as, what they want the family to be known for? What is the family story they want to tell?

5) Put your principles and values into a public format. List the three-to-five core principles. Make them memorable. I made a two-foot-by-three-foot canvas wall hanging for our principles, and added a Bible verse for each one. I have one list near the entrance of my house, one in my office, and one in my older kid's room. The DeKruyter Family Values list includes our mission statement, values, and principles, all over a large picture of a tree. If you like the idea, please run with it. I had a boss once who said in a tongue-in-cheek way, "Creativity is the ability to hide your sources." Feel free to be creative like me. I grabbed this idea from combining *Family ID* and Jay Link's book *Family Wealth* Counseling with advice from Lencioni's book.

6) Own it together. Display it in the house. Be proud of the work and journey taken to get to this spot. Talk about it regularly.

Laugh about mistakes and praise clear progress.

7) Use it in daily life. When correcting behavior, revisit the "Who We Are" spot. I've had my boys memorize the list at night before bed. And I often revisit the value "others first" after my kids are fighting.

8) And finally, change it when necessary. The first version will be good, but why not tweak every few years to make it really good? Each season and phase of life brings new challenges and will allow you to highlight new principles while downplaying others.

These are just a few steps you can take toward building a family legacy. You may want to combine this with reflection on your family history—how you and your spouse view your own families of origin, or how you came to be who you are today. When you reflect on the past and live with purpose toward the future, your time in the present becomes that much more meaningful.

## NOTES

### Prologue

[1] 1 Timothy 6:19 (English Standard Version)

### Chapter 1: The Difference Money Makes

[2] Graeme Wood, "Secret Fears of the Super Rich," *The Atlantic*, April, 2011, http://www.theatlantic.com/magazine/archive/2011/04/secret-fears-of-the-super-rich/308419/.

[3] Ibid.

### Chapter 2: Money and Your Heart

[4] "Charitable Giving in America: Some Facts and Figures," *National Center for Charitable Statistics*, accessed September 21, 2016, http://nccs.urban.org/nccs/statistics/Charitable-Giving-in-America-Some-Facts-and-Figures.cfm

[5] *Wikipedia*, s.v. "List of wealthiest historical figures," last modified September 18, 2016, https://en.wikipedia.org/wiki/List_of_wealthiest_historical_figures.

[6] Louis Hau, "What Worries the Rich," *Forbes*, May 23, 2007, http://www.forbes.com/2007/05/22/wealth-rich-poll-biz_cx_lh_0523worry.html

[7] Wood, "Secret Fears."

[8] Francis Chan, *Crazy Love*, rev. ed. (Colorado Springs, CO: David C. Cook, 2013).

### Chapter 3: Success, Achievement, and Significance

[9] John Maxwell, *The Journey from Success to Significance* (Nashville, TN: J Countryman, 2004), 9.

[10] Wayne's story can be found here: http://www.iamsecond.com/seconds/wayne-huizenga/

[11] Renee's story can be found here: https://vimeo.com/40037656

[12] Tom's story can be found here: http://www.cbsnews.com/video/watch/?id=3643660n

# APPENDIX B

[13] Janice's story can be found here: https://vimeo.com/87800468 or https://vimeo.com/63840258

[14] Andy Stanley, *How to Be Rich* (Grand Rapids, MI:: Zondervan, 2013).

[15] Robert Frank, *Richistan: A Journey Through the American Wealth Boom and the Lives of the New Rich* (New York: Crown Business, 2007).

[16] Laura Sanders, "Baby You're a Rich Man," *Wall Street Journal*, December 29, 2012.

### Chapter 4: Oh, the Lies we Tell Ourselves

[17] Barbara Blouin, "How One Inheritor Found Creative Ways to Overcome her Guilt and Shame," *The Inheritance Project Publications* (blog), October 26, 2015, http://inheritance-project.com/cms/?p=1638

### Chapter 5: Attacking the Root

[18] Neil Postman, *Amusing Ourselves to Death* (New York: Penguin Publishing Group, 1985).

### Chapter 7: The Flip Side of Affluence for Our Children

[19] *Born Rich*, directed by Jamie Johnson (2003), DVD.

[20] "Interview with Mother Teresa: A Pencil in the Hand of God," by Edward W. Desmond, *Time*, December 4, 1989.

### Chapter 8: Helping Our Kids Handle Money Well

[21] Po Bronson, "How Not to Talk to Your Kids," New York Magazine, August 3, 2007, http://nymag.com/news/features/27840/index2.html.

### Chapter 9: Beautiful Tension

[22] *Merriam-Webster Online*, s.v. "temperance," accessed September 23, 2016, http://www.merriam-webster.com/dictionary/temperance.

### Chapter 10: Community for the Affluent

[23] *Oxford Dictionaries*, s.v. "empathy," accessed September 22, 2016, https://en.oxforddictionaries.com/definition/empathy.